Big-Block Quilts
by MAGIC

- ◆ 30 Projects from Squares & Rectangles
- ◆ Features Easy & Accurate Diamond–Free® Technique
- ◆ 14 Bonus Quilting Designs

NANCY JOHNSON-SREBRO

C&T PUBLISHING

Text © 2006 Silver Star, Inc.

Artwork © 2006 C&T Publishing, Inc.

Publisher: Amy Marson

Editorial Director: Gailen Runge

Acquisitions Editor: Jan Grigsby

Editor: Liz Aneloski

Copy Editor/Technical Editors: Ellen Pahl and Wendy Mathson

Proofreader: Wordfirm Inc.

Design Director/Cover & Book Designer: Christina D. Jarumay

Illustrator: John Heisch

Production Assistant: Tim Manibusan

Photography: Diane Pedersen and Luke Mulks, unless otherwise noted

Published by C&T Publishing, Inc., P.O. Box 1456, Lafayette, CA, 94549

Front cover: *Tree of Life*, by Nancy Johnson-Srebro

Back cover: *Indian Puzzle* and *Carolina Lily All Grown Up*, by Nancy Johnson-Srebro

Library of Congress Cataloging-in-Publication Data

Johnson-Srebro, Nancy.

  Big-block quilts by magic : 30 projects from squares & rectangles,

features easy & accurate diamond-free technique, 14 bonus quilting designs /

Nancy Johnson-Srebro.

     p. cm.

  ISBN-13: 978-1-57120-308-3 (paper trade)

  ISBN-10: 1-57120-308-7 (paper trade)

  1. Patchwork--Patterns. 2. Quilting--Patterns. 3. Patchwork quilts. I.Title.

  TT835.J5858 2006

  746.46'041--dc22

                    2006002798

Printed in China
10 9 8 7 6 5 4 3 2 1

No-Fail®, Quilt Map®, and Diamond-Free® are registered trademarks of Silver Star, Inc.

IMPORTANT LEGAL NOTICE:

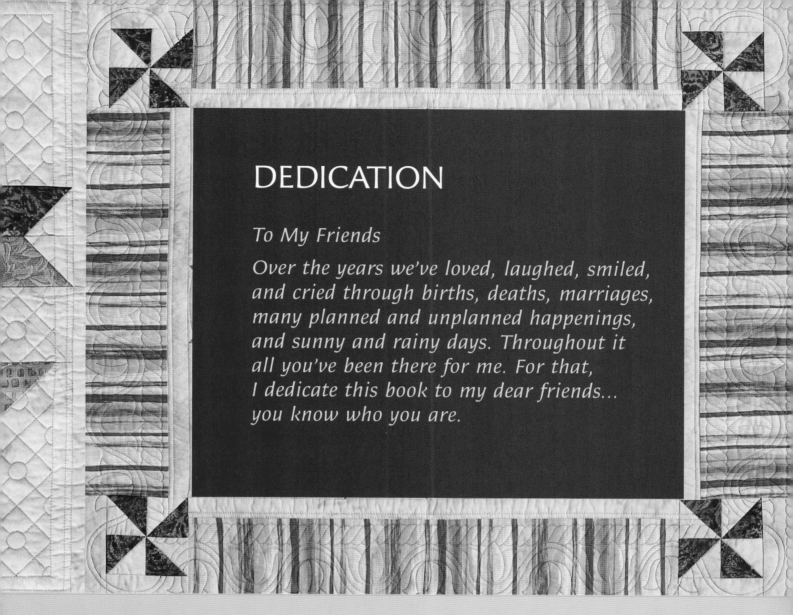

DEDICATION

To My Friends

Over the years we've loved, laughed, smiled, and cried through births, deaths, marriages, many planned and unplanned happenings, and sunny and rainy days. Throughout it all you've been there for me. For that, I dedicate this book to my dear friends... you know who you are.

ACKNOWLEDGMENTS

To my quilt team—Karen Bolesta, Karen Brown, Cindy Cochran, Debbie Donowski, Beth Anne Lowrie, Janet McCarroll, Vicki Novajosky, Ellen Pahl, Marcia Rickansrud, and Rocky Sidorek—you're the best!

Special thanks to master quilters Veronica Nurmi and Cindy Needham. I couldn't have done this book without your superb machine quilting talents.

A big Thank You to my editors, Liz Aneloski and Ellen Pahl, and to the entire C&T Staff.

Thanks also to Kaiser. You brought unexpected joy to our lives.

Last, but certainly not least, I offer a sincere Thank You to the following companies whose products were used in this book.

American & Efird	Bernina of America	Fairfield Processing Corporation	FreeSpirit
Hobbs Bonded Fibers	Mountain Mist	P&B Textiles	Prym Consumer USA, Inc.
Quilting Creations International	RJR Fashion Fabrics	Robert Kaufman Co., Inc.	Superior Threads
Timeless Treasures	The Warm Company		

CONTENTS

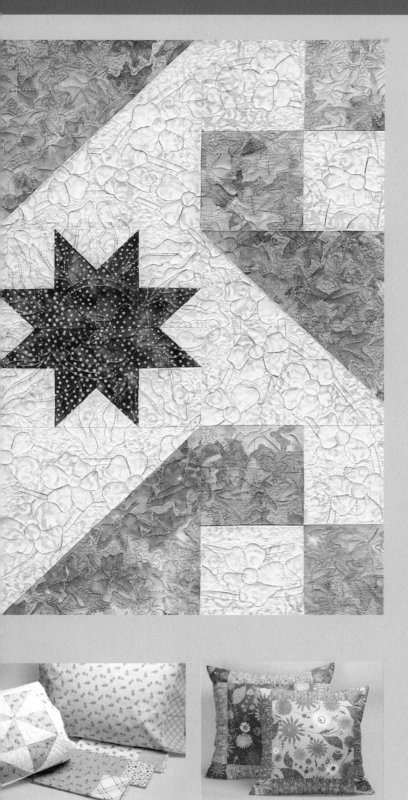

INTRODUCTION

Have you ever started a simple project for your home and the next thing you know it's become much larger? Like deciding to plant some new flowers in front along your sidewalk and the next thing you know you're leaving the garden center with your trunk full of flowers, shrubs, bags of dirt, tools, etc. Well, that's how this book came about. After using my grandma Garrison's antique full-size bed for over 25 years, we decided to buy a queen-size bed. It was a simple change. But the next thing I knew, I didn't have any quilts that looked right for our new bed, and I have over 50 to choose from!

The blocks in my full-size quilts were lost on the larger mattress. Our new queen-size mattress was telling me, "I need big blocks in the quilt to look good." What's a quilter to do? You already know the answer. I dug out my graph paper and cutting equipment and started making some new quilts with "big blocks." The next thing I knew, I was working on another book!

Originally I thought I could just add another row of 12″ blocks to my existing patterns, but I soon found out that this didn't look right. The design of the blocks looked lost on such a large mattress. The size differ-ence between a queen/king and full-size bed just seems to demand a proportional increase in the size of the blocks, not just adding more of them! Plus, who wants to make 25 or 30 blocks for one quilt?

The patterns in this book are so quick and easy you can make a wallhanging in a few hours and the bed-size *Carolina Lily* quilt takes only 4 big blocks! Of course, all the quilts use only squares and rectangles. No fancy cutting or complicated piecing! What could be simpler than that?

Enjoy!

How to Read The Charts

Each quilt project includes a complete yardage chart, cutting chart, and quilt map, along with piecing directions for blocks and other units.

Letters refer to specific pieces of the quilt map	Color as it appears in the featured quilt	Yardage needed

YARDAGE

ITEM	COLOR	QUANTITY NEEDED
Star (A), *Flat Piping	■	1/4 yard
Star Background (B, C)	□	1 1/4 yards
Triangle Unit (D)		
4-Patch (E), *Borders		
4-Patch (F)	■	1/2 yard
Triangle Unit (G)		
Binding	■	1/2 yard
Backing		40" × 40"

*Based on cutting crosswise grain of the fabric.

CUTTING

ITEM	COLOR	# TO CUT	SIZE
A	■	8	2 1/8" × 4 1/2"
B	□	8	2 7/8" × 4 1/2"
C	□	8	2 1/8"
D	□	2	8 7/8" × 8 7/8"
E	□	1	4 1/2" × 40"
F	■	1	4 1/2" × 40"
G	■	2	8 7/8" × 8 7/8"
Flat Piping	■	4	1" × 24 1/2"
Side Borders	□	2	5 1/4" × 24 1/2"
Top/Bottom Borders	□	2	5 1/4" × 34"

The cutting charts for the quilts list the cut size of each piece, in inches. Single measurements indicate the size of a cut square (5" = 5" × 5").

Yardage and cutting charts are provided with each quilt map. I've overestimated the yardage needed by a small factor to allow for preshrinking the fabric and squaring up. I didn't give the exact length for cutting the borders for the lap/queen/king size quilts. I've given you the number of strips to cut on the crosswise grain; you will need to measure your quilt top, piece the strips using a straight seam, and trim to the size of your quilt.

I allowed for 3" strips when cutting binding even though I usually cut 2 1/8" strips for double-fold binding. The backing is 6" larger than the size of the quilt. The backing should be 10" larger than the size of the quilt if you are going to quilt with a longarm machine. Batting should be the same size as the backing. All yardage for the quilts and accent pillows is based on 40"-wide fabric after washing and removing selvages. However, note that the pillowcases require fabric that is at least 42" wide after washing and removing selvages.

Rotary Cutting Equipment

ROTARY CUTTERS

Be sure to use a rotary cutter that is suited to your personal style and physical needs. I've found that either the Dritz 45mm or Omnigrid 45mm pressure-sensitive rotary cutter allows me to rotary cut for hours without hand fatigue.

RULERS

Use accurately printed rulers, such as Omnigrip products. I found the Diamond-Free 6″ × 14″, 8½″ × 24″, and the 20½″ square Omnigrip rulers were most helpful when cutting out the big blocks.

CUTTING MATS

I prefer the Omnigrid mat in particular because it's reversible —green on one side and light gray on the other side. I use the light gray side of the mat for cutting because it provides higher contrast between medium and dark fabrics and the color of the mat.

 MY FAVORITE THINGS

If your ruler slips while rotary cutting, place a sheet of Invisigrip on the back of the ruler. This product will prevent your ruler from slipping. It also works great on the bottom of templates!

No-Fail Rotary Cutting

There are only two shapes used in the Big Block patterns in this book—a square and a rectangle. Both are very easy to rotary cut. The photos that follow in this section show the cutting technique for a left-handed and a right-handed person.

CUTTING A SQUARE

Step One

The cutting charts for the blocks and quilts give the cut measurement of a square. This will determine the width of the strip you will cut. For example, if the instructions require three 4″ × 4″ squares, cut a strip of fabric 4″ wide and 13″ long. Always cut the strip a little longer than necessary; this will allow you to "square up" the short end of the strip. Place the short side of the ruler along the top of the strip. Square up the short side of the strip by cutting approximately ¼″ from the edge.

Left-Handed   *Right-Handed*

Step Two

After squaring up one end of the strip, turn the mat one-half turn (180°). Place the ruler on top of the fabric so the 4″ marking aligns with the newly cut edge. Be sure the top of the ruler is even with the top of the strip. Firmly hold the ruler with one hand and cut along the edge of the ruler with your rotary cutter.

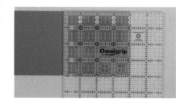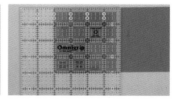

Left-Handed   *Right-Handed*

 NO-FAIL CUTTING TIP

Be sure you always press your fabric before cutting any shape. If you use wrinkled fabric, the cut shapes will grow in size after you press the wrinkles out.

CUTTING A RECTANGLE

The cutting charts give the cut dimensions for the rectangle. Use the smaller dimension to determine the width of the strip you will cut. Let's say the cutting instructions call for two 4″ × 6″ rectangles. Cut a strip of fabric 4″ wide and 13″ long; this allows an extra inch for squaring up. Square up the short end of the strip as shown in Step One of Cutting a Square. Turn the mat one-half turn. Next, place the ruler on top of the strip so the 6″ marking aligns with the newly cut edge. Be sure the top of the ruler is even with the top of the strip. Rotary cut.

 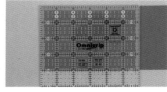

Left-Handed	Right-Handed

Sewing and Pressing

Sewing quilt blocks has never been easier! Straight sewing is all that's required even for blocks like the Carolina Lily or Tree of Life. In this section I will share some of my special hints and tips for making these quick and easy big blocks.

SEAM ALLOWANCE

I find it's best to use a scant ¼″ seam allowance (unless otherwise noted) when piecing quilts. Using a scant seam allowance ensures that the units and blocks are true to size because you regain the small amount of fabric that is lost due to the thickness of the sewing thread and the resulting "hump" that's created by pressing the seam allowances to one side.

 My Favorite Things

For accurate sewing, use fine silk pins when pinning your pieces together. Try using C104 Collins Silk Pins by Prym Consumer USA, Inc.

NO-FAIL TIPS FOR SEWING ON THE DIAGONAL

- When working with squares and rectangles, sometimes you need to draw a thin pencil line diagonally through the piece in order to sew it to the next piece. DO NOT sew precisely on the drawn pencil line. Sew one or two thread widths to the right of it to obtain a scant ¼″ seam allowance. This ensures that the piece will be the correct size after pressing. If you sew exactly on the pencil line, the piece will likely be too small after pressing.

Stitch to the right of the pencil line.

- Use a mechanical pencil with a lead no more than 0.5mm in diameter for drawing diagonal lines on light fabric, and use an ultra-fine-point black Sharpie for dark fabrics. Do not use a regular pencil. It will become dull very quickly and the pencil line will be wider and bolder than desired.

- Keep sharp needles in your sewing machine. A dull needle will distort the first few stitches.

- A single-hole or straight-stitch plate is also helpful. It keeps the needle from pushing the corner of the square into the zigzag throat-plate hole (which has a larger opening).

- When sewing diagonally through a square or rectangle, start sewing on a scrap piece of fabric first, then continue sewing into the adjacent square/rectangle. This will help prevent distortion of the first one or two stitches.

- Try piecing with an open-toe walking foot. The open toe will allow you to see where to sew NEXT to the pencil line. The walking foot ensures that the two layers of fabric will feed through evenly. I do all my machine piecing on a Bernina with an open-toe walking foot.

- The needle-stop down feature on the sewing machine is very helpful when chain piecing. It keeps the fabric in place when you stop sewing momentarily. Use this feature if your machine has it.

- Press the diagonally sewn seam flat to "set" the stitches. This prevents distortion of the seam and pieces. Next press the seam allowance to one side. Then trim off the excess fabric.

SEWING WITH SQUARES AND RECTANGLES

There are several quick and easy methods I've used to make the quilts in this book. They're accurate and great time-savers. Once you try them, I'm sure you'll find that your quilts go together easier and faster than ever before.

HOW TO CREATE ONE PIECED SQUARE
Step One

Begin with two same-size squares cut as directed for the block you are making. Draw a diagonal line from corner to corner on the WRONG SIDE of one square. With right sides together, place that square on top of the other square.

Stitch one or two thread widths to the right of the pencil line. Press the square according to the pressing arrows in the block instructions.

Draw a line, stitch, and press.

Step Two

Carefully lay the sewn pieces on a cutting mat. Using a ruler and rotary cutter, cut ¼″ away from the stitching line. You will have two triangle-shaped pieces of fabric left over. Discard these pieces or save them for future projects.

Trim.

HOW TO CREATE TWO PIECED SQUARES
Step One

Begin with two squares of equal size cut as directed for the block you are making. Draw a diagonal line from corner to corner on the WRONG SIDE of the lighter square. Next draw a diagonal line ¼″ away from and parallel to the first diagonal line. Do the same on the opposite side of the first

diagonal line. With right sides together, position the lighter square on top of the darker square.

Draw pencil lines.

Step Two

Sew one or two thread widths on the inside of the outermost pencil lines. Using a ruler and rotary cutter, cut along the center diagonal pencil line. Press.

Sew just inside the pencil lines.

✦ MY FAVORITE THINGS

Try the Diamond-Free Omnigrip ruler to trim the ¼″ seam allowance more easily and quickly than you ever thought possible. The highlighted ¼″ vertical area on the ruler will eliminate any cutting errors. It will also work great when you need to draw stitching lines exactly ¼″ away from a diagonal line when creating two pieced squares (as in Step One bottom left).

SEWING ON THE DIAGONAL USING A SQUARE AND A RECTANGLE
Step One

On the WRONG SIDE of the fabric, draw a diagonal line across the square. With right sides together, place the square on the rectangle. Stitch one or two thread widths to the right of the pencil line.

Draw a line, align, and stitch.

Step Two

Press the square according to the pressing arrows in the block instructions. Carefully lay the pieces on a cutting mat. Using a ruler and rotary cutter, trim ¼″ away from the stitching line. Discard or save the two triangle-shaped pieces of fabric.

Press and trim.

SEWING ON THE DIAGONAL USING TWO RECTANGLES

Step One

In order to draw a pencil line on a rectangle, position the top rectangle a little away from the edge of the rectangle that is beneath it.

Align the top edge of the upper rectangle with the top edge of the lower rectangle. This allows you to see where to draw the diagonal pencil line. Draw a pencil line from the upper corner diagonally to where the rectangles meet (45°).

Align and draw a line.

Step Two

Move the top rectangle so the edges of the two rectangles are even. Sew, press, and trim ¼″ from the stitching line.

Align and sew.   *Stitch and trim.*

✦ MY FAVORITE THINGS

For a really nice-looking stitch, trying using a Schmetz Jeans/Denim, 70/10 needle. Don't be fooled by the words Jeans/Denim. The point of this needle is very sharp and will give you a perfect looking top and bobbin stitch.

NO-FAIL PRESSING TIPS

I've been talking about and demonstrating good pressing habits since 1987. I truly believe that careful pressing is one of the reasons I've been able to make award-winning quilts. I feel so strongly about this part of quiltmaking that I've always included pressing arrows with my patterns. This book is no different. I've included pressing arrows with the block diagrams. These are only suggestions but are highly recommended. If you follow these pressing arrows, you should be able to butt most of your pieces together to accurately align and stitch them together. This will help keep your blocks square.

Here are a few other pressing tips:

- Be sure to press each seam allowance before continuing to sew more pieces to the unit.

- I normally don't use steam when quiltmaking. I find that it tends to distort many of the smaller pieces. If you use steam, be extra careful while pressing.

- Use the cotton setting on your iron. If this doesn't seem hot enough, set it one notch higher. After you press a piece, it should lie fairly flat on the ironing board.

- To get stubborn seam allowances to lie flat, place a tiny piece of ¼″-wide Steam-A-Seam 2 under the seam allowance and press. This will fuse the seam allowance in place.

Fabric and Thread Choices

My machine quilters often ask me how I get my quilt tops to lie so flat and square. This means the top edge is the same length as the bottom edge of the quilt, and both sides of the quilt are the same length. One of the reasons for this is the quality of the fabrics I use. Working with tightly woven, good-quality 100% cotton fabric will help keep your quilt tops square. Loosely woven fabrics will allow your quilt blocks to stretch more easily while sewing and quilting on them. You'll make your machine quilters very happy if your quilt tops are square!

If possible, prewash the fabrics before using them. This ensures that the fabrics are preshrunk and the dyes won't bleed if your block or quilt must be washed in the future.

All of my machine piecing is done with Mettler 100% cotton, silk-finish thread. The weight is 50/3. For most of my piecing I use a light beige color thread (color #703 or #810).

INDIAN PUZZLE

Indian Puzzle Wallhanging made by Nancy Johnson-Srebro.

Quilted by Veronica Nurmi.

Quilt Size: 34″ × 34″

Finished Big Block Size: 24″ × 24″

Finished Star, 4-Patch, and Half-Square Triangle Units size: 8″ × 8″

You can sew this wallhanging in a few hours! The 8-Pointed Star in the center adds extra movement to this easy pattern along with a bit of sophistication.

 NO-FAIL TIP

Pay close attention to the placement of the 4-patch and half-square triangle units. It's easy to get them turned the wrong way.

Option A

Quilting Designs

Quilting options by Veronica Nurmi.

Option B

Note: See page 95 for stencil information.

INDIAN PUZZLE WALLHANGING

Size: 34″ × 34″

Big Blocks Needed: 1

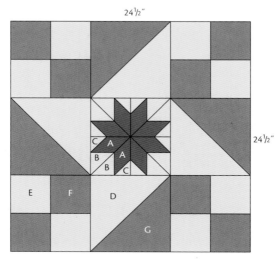

24½″

24½″

Big Block

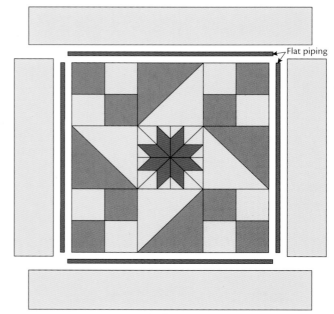

Flat piping

Quilt Map

Complete Diagram

YARDAGE

ITEM	COLOR	QUANTITY NEEDED
Star (A), *Flat Piping		¹⁄₄ yard
Star Background (B, C)		1¹⁄₄ yards
Triangle Unit (D)		
4-Patch (E), *Borders		
4-Patch (F)		¹⁄₂ yard
Triangle Unit (G)		
Binding		¹⁄₂ yard
Backing		40″ × 40″

*Based on cutting crosswise grain of the fabric.

CUTTING

ITEM	COLOR	# TO CUT	SIZE
A		8	2¹⁄₈″ × 4¹⁄₂″
B		8	2⁷⁄₈″ × 4¹⁄₂″
C		8	2¹⁄₈″
D		2	8⁷⁄₈″ × 8⁷⁄₈″
E		1	4¹⁄₂″ × 40″
F		1	4¹⁄₂″ × 40″
G		2	8⁷⁄₈″ × 8⁷⁄₈″
Flat Piping		4	1″ × 24¹⁄₂″
Side Borders		2	5¹⁄₄″ × 24¹⁄₂″
Top/Bottom Borders		2	5¹⁄₄″ × 34″

NOTE: For sewing instructions, see pages 15–17. Refer to the diagrams at left for the number of units and blocks needed.

8-Pointed Star;
Make 1.

4-Patch;
Make 4.

Half-Square
Triangle Unit;
Make 4.

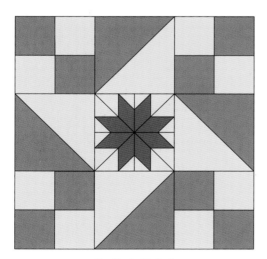

Big Block; Make 1.

Sewing the Blocks and Units

8-Pointed Star

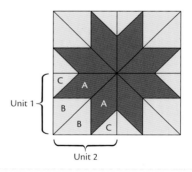

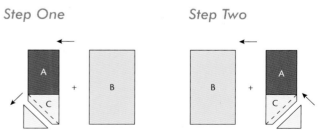

Step One   *Step Two*

Unit 1; Make 4.   *Unit 2; Make 4.*

Step Three

Draw a diagonal line on the WRONG SIDE of all Unit 2s, as shown. Place Unit 2, WRONG SIDE up, on top of Unit 1. Align, sew, press, and trim.

Step Four

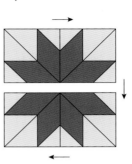

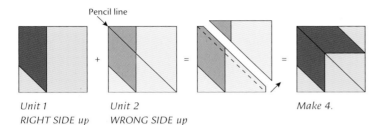

Pencil line

Unit 1
RIGHT SIDE up

Unit 2
WRONG SIDE up

Make 4.

4-Patch Unit

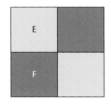

E

F

Step One

Sew strip E to strip F. Cut into 4½″ sections.

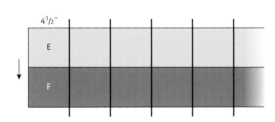

4½″

E

F

Wallhanging: Cut 8. Lap: Cut 18. Queen/King: Cut 72.

Step Two

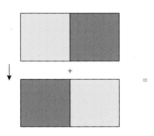

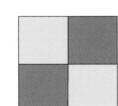

Half-Square Triangle Unit

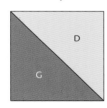

D

G

Step One

On the WRONG SIDE of the light (D) square, draw a pencil line diagonally from corner to corner. Draw a line ¼″ away from the first pencil line on both sides.

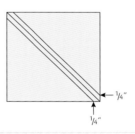

¼″

¼″

Step Two

Place the (D) square on top of the (G) square, right sides together. Sew a couple of thread widths on the inside of the second and third pencil lines. Using a ruler and rotary cutter, cut through the first pencil line. Cut off the dog ears and press toward the dark. This method will yield 2 half-square triangle blocks.

Stitch

Cut

Dog ears

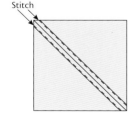

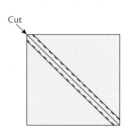

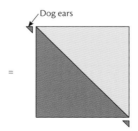

=

Block Assembly

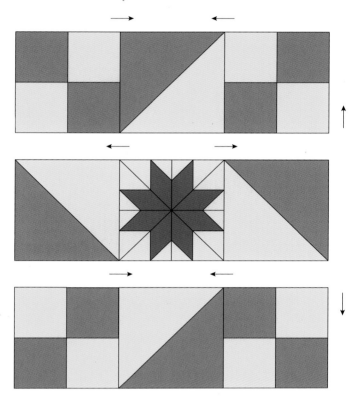

Flat Piping

Wallhanging: Cut 1″-wide strips.

Lap and Queen/King: Cut 1½″-wide strips.

Sew the short ends of the strips together if needed. Press the strips in half lengthwise with wrong sides together. Trim these strips to the length and width of the quilt and follow the sewing diagrams. The 1″ strips will be ¼″ finished and the 1½″ strips will be ½″.

Step One

Align the raw edges of the piping with the sides of the quilt. Stitch, using a very scant ¼″ seam.

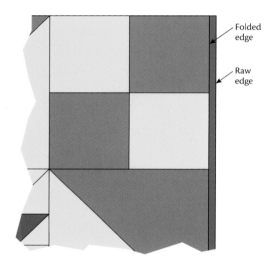

Step Two

Align the raw edges of the piping with the top/bottom edges of the quilt. Stitch.

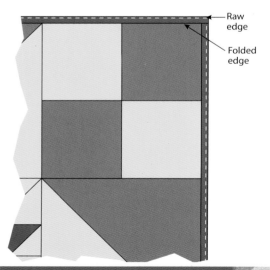

INDIAN PUZZLE LAP QUILT

(See photo on page 89.)

Size: 52″ × 52″
Big Blocks Needed: 1

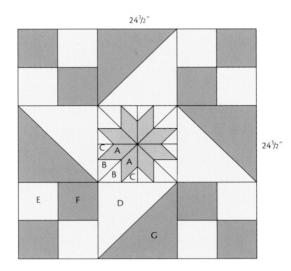

Big Block

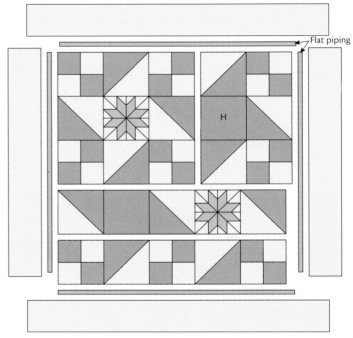

Quilt Map

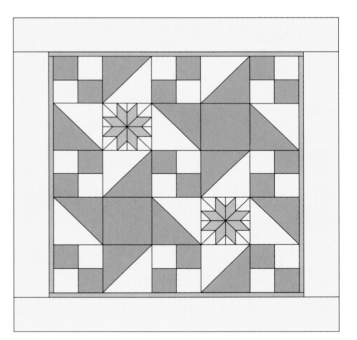

Complete Diagram

YARDAGE

ITEM	COLOR	QUANTITY NEEDED
Star (A), *Flat Piping	▨	½ yard
Star Background (B, C)	☐	2⅜ yards
Triangle Unit (D)		
4-Patch (E), *Borders		
4-Patch (F)	▨	1¼ yards
Triangle Unit (G)		
Solid Block (H)		
Binding	▨	⅝ yard
Backing		58″ × 58″

*Based on cutting crosswise grain of the fabric. You will need to piece these strips to get the length required.

CUTTING

ITEM	COLOR	# TO CUT	SIZE
A	▨	16	2⅛″ × 4½″
B	☐	16	2⅞″ × 4½″
C	☐	16	2⅛″
D	☐	6	8⅞″ × 8⅞″
E	☐	3	4½″ × 40″
F	▨	3	4½″ × 40″
G	▨	6	8⅞″ × 8⅞″
H	▨	2	8½″ × 8½″
Flat Piping	▨	5	1½″ × 40″
Borders	☐	6	6¼″ × 40″

NOTE: For sewing instructions, see pages 15–17. Refer to the diagrams at right for the number of blocks and units needed.

8-Pointed Star; Make 2.

4-Patch; Make 9.

Half-Square Triangle Unit; Make 12.

Big Block; Make 1.

INDIAN PUZZLE QUEEN/KING QUILT

Queen: 98″ × 98″

King: 104″ × 104″

Big Blocks Needed: 9

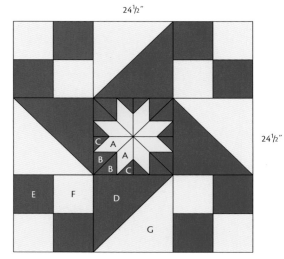

Big Block

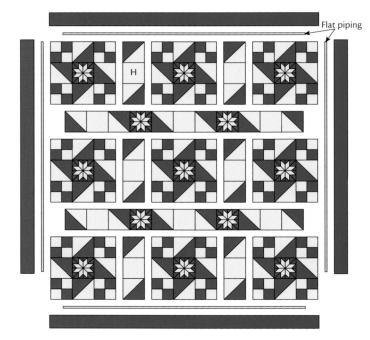

Quilt Map

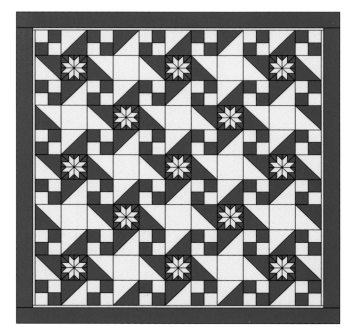

Complete Diagram

YARDAGE

ITEM	COLOR	QUEEN	KING
		Quantity Needed	
Star (A), *Flat Piping	⬜	1½ yards	1½ yards
Star Background (B, C)	🟥	6¾ yards	8 yards
Triangle Block (D)			
4-Patch (E), *Borders			
4-Patch (F)	⬜	4⅛ yards	4⅛ yards
Triangle Block (G)			
Solid Block (H)			
Binding	🟥	1⅛ yards	1⅛ yards
Backing		104″ × 104″	110″ × 110″

*Based on cutting crosswise grain of the fabric. You will need to piece these strips to get the length required.

CUTTING for Queen and King

ITEM	COLOR	# TO CUT	SIZE
A	⬜	104	2⅛″ × 4½″
B	🟥	104	2⅞″ × 4½″
C	🟥	104	2⅛″
D	🟥	30	8⅞″ × 8⅞″
E	🟥	9	4½″ × 40″
F	⬜	9	4½″ × 40″
G	⬜	30	8⅞″ × 8⅞″
H	⬜	12	8½″ × 8½″
Flat Piping	⬜	9	1½″ × 40″
Queen Borders	🟥	10	5¼″ × 40″
King Borders	🟥	11	8¼″ × 40″

NOTE: For sewing instructions, see pages 15–17. Refer to the diagrams at right for the number of blocks and units needed.

8-Pointed Star; Make 13.

4-Patch; Make 36.

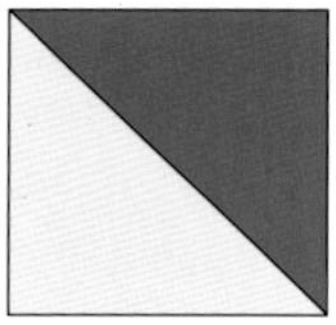

Half-Square Triangle Unit; Make 60.

Big Block; Make 9.

RICK RACK AND ROLL

Rick Rack and Roll Wallhanging made by Nancy Johnson-Srebro.

Quilted by Cindy Needham.

Quilt Size: 36$\frac{1}{2}$″ × 36$\frac{1}{2}$″

Finished Big Block Size: 24″ × 24″

Finished Star and Rickrack Block Size: 8″ × 8″

I like the way the Rickrack block twists, turns, and rolls around the simple Variable Stars. Gather up lots of scraps for the stars and see how easy this wallhanging is to make.

 ## NO-FAIL TIPS

■ *To balance the colors on the queen-size quilt (photo page 92), I suggest that you sew all of the Rick Rack blocks and half of the Star blocks. Arrange them on a design wall. Then, you can determine how many of the remaining star blocks should be light or dark to complement the already sewn blocks.*

■ *Make sure you have the Rickrack block facing in the correct direction when sewing it to the star block. The "double" points face toward the center square.*

■ *Using many different shades of one color for the stars will add a lot of interest and texture to your quilt.*

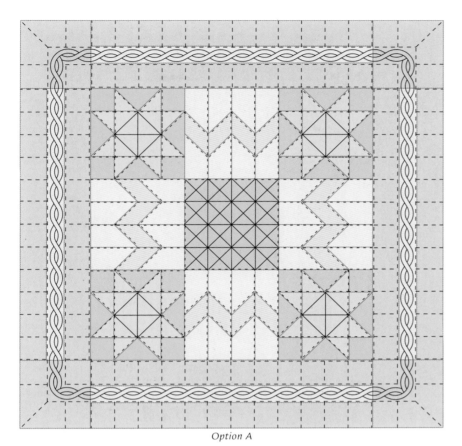

Option A

Quilting Designs

Quilting options by Cindy Needham.

Note: See page 95 for stencil information.

Option B

RICK RACK AND ROLL WALLHANGING

Size: $36^1/2'' \times 36^1/2''$

Big Blocks Needed: 1

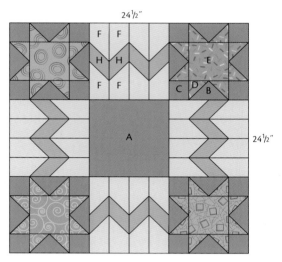

24½"

24½"

Big Block

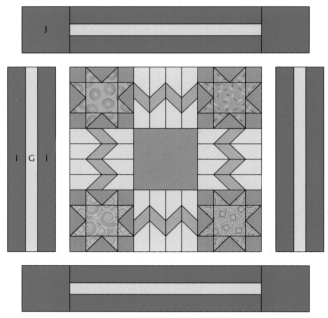

Quilt Map

Complete Diagram

YARDAGE

ITEM	COLOR	QUANTITY NEEDED
A, Star Background (B, C)		½ yard
Star (D, E)		8″ × 18″ strip of 4 different fabrics
Rick Rack Background (F), Border (*G)		⅝ yard
Rick Rack (H)		¼ yard
Border (*I), Cornerstones (J)		⅞ yard
Binding		½ yard
Backing		43″ × 43″

*Based on cutting crosswise grain of the fabric.

CUTTING

ITEM	COLOR	# TO CUT	SIZE
A		1	8½″ × 8½″
B		16	2½″ × 4½″
C		16	2½″ × 2½″
*D		8	2½″ × 2½″
*E		1	4½″ × 4½″
F		32	2½″ × 4½″
G		4	2″ × 24½″
H		16	2½″ × 4½″
I		8	2¾″ × 24½″
J		4	6½″ × 6½″

*Cut from each of the 4 fabrics.

NOTE: For sewing instructions, see page 26. Refer to the diagrams at right for the number of blocks and units needed.

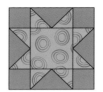

Variable Star; Make 4.

Rickrack Unit; Make 4.

Big Block; Make 1.

Border Strip Set; Make 4.

Sewing the Blocks and Units

VARIABLE STAR

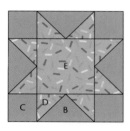

Step One

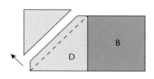

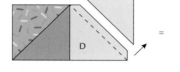

Make 4.

Step Two

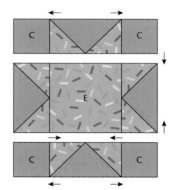

RICKRACK BLOCK

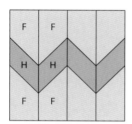

Rickrack Block

Step One

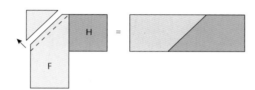

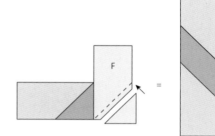

Unit 1; Make 2.

Step Two

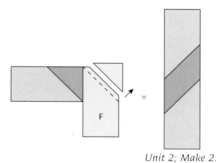

Unit 2; Make 2.

Step Three

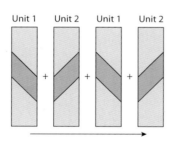

Unit 1   Unit 2   Unit 1   Unit 2

BIG BLOCK ASSEMBLY

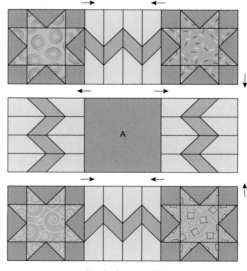

Big Block Assembly

RICK RACK AND ROLL LAP QUILT

Size: 64″ × 64″

Big Blocks Needed: 4

24½″

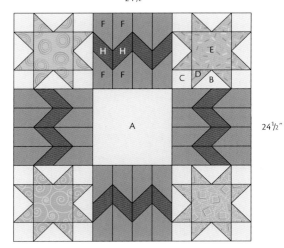

24½″

Big Block

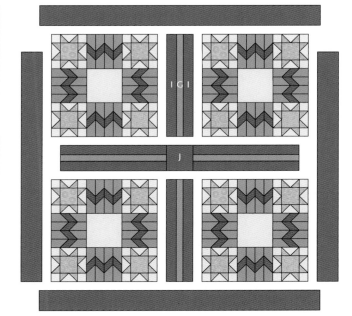

Quilt Map

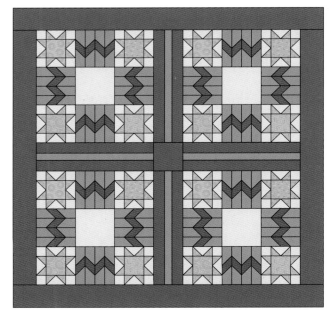

Complete Diagram

YARDAGE

ITEM	COLOR	QUANTITY NEEDED
A, Star Background (B, C)		1 3/8 yards
Star (D, E)		8″ × 18″ strip of 16 different fabrics
Rick Rack Background (F), Lattice (*G)		1 1/2 yards
Rick Rack (H)		3/4 yard
Lattice (*I), Cornerstone (J), *Borders		2 yards
Binding		3/4 yard
Backing		70″ × 70″

*Based on cutting crosswise grain of the fabric. You will need to piece the borders to get the length required.

CUTTING

ITEM	COLOR	# TO CUT	SIZE
A		4	8 1/2″ × 8 1/2″
B		64	2 1/2″ × 4 1/2″
C		64	2 1/2″ × 2 1/2″
*D		8	2 1/2″ × 2 1/2″
*E		1	4 1/2″ × 4 1/2″
F		128	2 1/2″ × 4 1/2″
G		4	2″ × 24 1/2″
H		64	2 1/2″ × 4 1/2″
I		8	2 3/4″ × 24 1/2″
J		1	6 1/2″ × 6 1/2″
Borders		7	5 1/4″ × 40″

*Cut from each of the 16 fabrics.

NOTE: For sewing instructions, see page 26. Refer to the diagrams at right for the number of blocks and units needed.

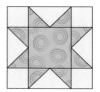

Variable Star; Make 16.

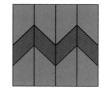

Rickrack Unit; Make 16.

Big Block; Make 4.

Lattice Strip Set; Make 4.

RICK RACK AND ROLL QUEEN/KING QUILT

(See photo on page 92.)

Queen: 96″ × 96″

King: 104″ × 104″

Big Blocks Needed: 9

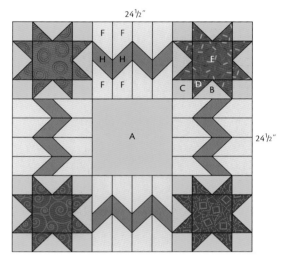

Big Block

Vertical Sashing

Horizontal Sashing

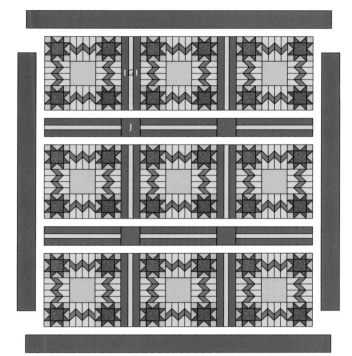

Quilt Map

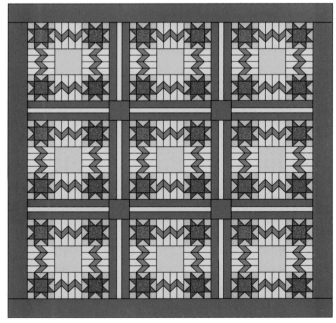

Complete Diagram

YARDAGE

ITEM	COLOR	Quantity Needed	
		QUEEN	**KING**
A, Star Background (B, C)		$2^3/_4$ yards	$2^3/_4$ yards
Star (D, E)		$8'' \times 18''$ strip of 36 different fabrics	$8'' \times 18''$ strip of 36 different fabrics
Rick Rack Background (F), Lattice (*G)		$3^1/_4$ yards	$3^1/_4$ yards
Rick Rack (H)		$1^3/_8$ yards	$1^3/_8$ yards
Lattice (*I), J, *Borders		4 yards	$5^1/_4$ yards
Binding		I yard	$1^1/_8$ yards
Backing		$102'' \times 102''$	$110'' \times 110''$

*Based on cutting crosswise grain of the fabric. You will need to piece the borders to get the length required.

CUTTING for Queen and King

ITEM	COLOR	# TO CUT	SIZE
A		9	$8^1/_2'' \times 8^1/_2''$
B		144	$2^1/_2'' \times 4^1/_2''$
C		144	$2^1/_2'' \times 2^1/_2''$
*D		8	$2^1/_2'' \times 2^1/_2''$
*E		I	$4^1/_2'' \times 4^1/_2''$
F		288	$2^1/_2'' \times 4^1/_2''$
G		12	$2'' \times 24^1/_2''$
H		144	$2^1/_2'' \times 4^1/_2''$
I		24	$2^3/_4'' \times 24^1/_2''$
J		4	$6^1/_2'' \times 6^1/_2''$
Queen Borders		10	$6^1/_4'' \times 40''$
King Borders		11	$10^1/_4'' \times 40''$

*Cut from each of the 36 fabrics.

NOTE: For sewing instructions, see page 26. Refer to the diagrams at right for the number of blocks and units needed.

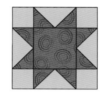

Variable Star; Make 36.

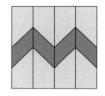

Rickrack Unit; Make 36.

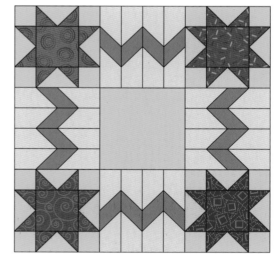

Big Block; Make 9.

Lattice Strip Set; Make 12.

HOME SWEET HOME

Home Sweet Home Wallhanging made by Nancy Johnson-Srebro.

Quilted by Veronica Nurmi.

Quilt Size: 46″ × 46″

Finished Big Block Size: 18″ × 18″

Finished Tree Block Size: 9″ × 9″

Here's a chance to use lots of those fun background fabrics you've been collecting! The big and bold house will stand out nicely against a scrappy background. Plant tree blocks in each corner—make them all the same, as I did, or choose different fabrics for each.

 NO-FAIL TIP

If using shades of one color, such as beige, make sure the background fabric around the house block is several shades lighter or darker than the surrounding background squares. Otherwise the house block won't stand out.

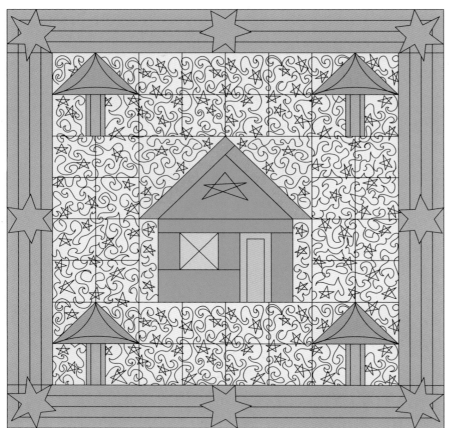

Option A

Quilting Designs

Quilting options by Veronica Nurmi.

Note: See page 95 for stencil information.

Option B

HOME SWEET HOME WALLHANGING

Size: 46″ × 46″

Big Blocks Needed: 1

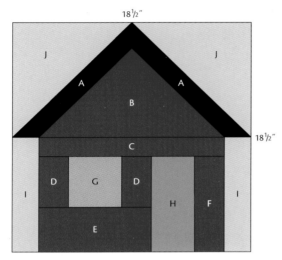

Big Block

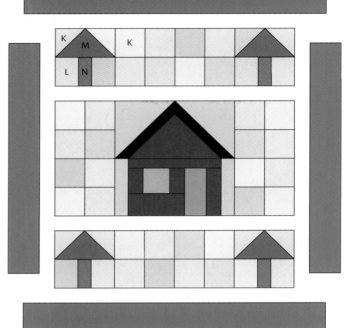

Quilt Map

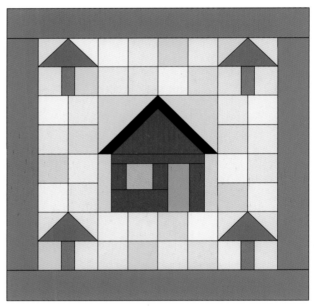

Complete Diagram

YARDAGE

ITEM	COLOR	QUANTITY NEEDED
Roof (A)	⬛	³⁄₈ yard
House (B, C, D, E, F)	⬛	³⁄₈ yard
Window (G)	⬛	6″ × 6″ square
Door (H)	⬛	6″ × 10″ rectangle
House Background (I, J)	⬛	¹⁄₂ yard
Background (K, L)	▥	¹⁄₄ yard of 8 different fabrics
Tree Top (M)	⬛	¹⁄₄ yard
Tree Trunk (N)	⬛	¹⁄₈ yard
*Borders	⬛	1 yard
Binding	⬛	⁵⁄₈ yard
Backing		52″ × 52″

*Based on cutting crosswise grain of the fabric. You will need to piece the top/bottom border strips to get the length required.

CUTTING

ITEM	COLOR	# TO CUT	SIZE
A	⬛	2	9¹⁄₂″ × 11¹⁄₂″
B	⬛	1	9¹⁄₂″ × 14¹⁄₂″
C	⬛	1	2″ × 14¹⁄₂″
D	⬛	2	2³⁄₄″ × 4¹⁄₂″
E	⬛	1	4″ × 9″
F	⬛	1	2³⁄₄″ × 8″
G	⬛	1	4¹⁄₂″ × 4¹⁄₂″
H	⬛	1	3³⁄₄″ × 8″
I	⬛	2	2¹⁄₂″ × 9¹⁄₂″
J	⬛	2	9¹⁄₂″ × 9¹⁄₂″
*K	▥	5	5″ × 5″
*L	▥	1	4″ × 5″
M	⬛	4	5″ × 9¹⁄₂″
N	⬛	4	2¹⁄₂″ × 5″
Side Borders	⬛	2	5¹⁄₄″ × 36¹⁄₂″
Top/Bottom Borders	⬛	4	5¹⁄₄″ × 23¹⁄₄″

* Cut from each of the 8 fabrics.

NOTE: For sewing instructions, see page 35. Refer to the diagrams at left for the number of blocks needed.

Tree; Make 4.

Big Block; Make 1.

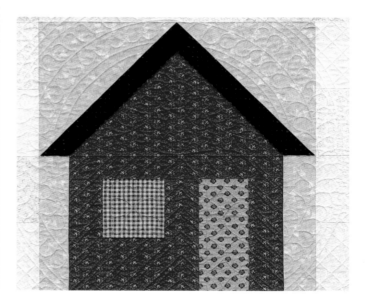

Sewing the Blocks

Big Block

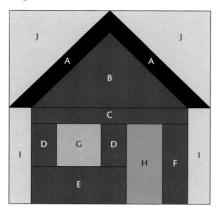

Step One

Step One

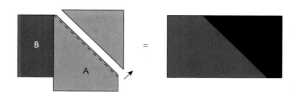

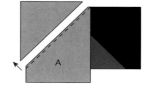

Step Two

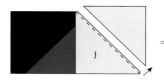

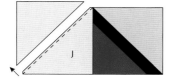

Step Three

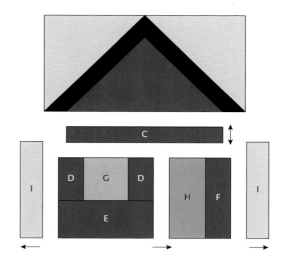

Tree

Step Two

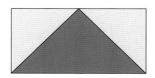

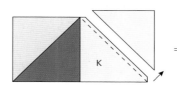

Step One

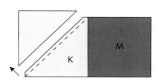

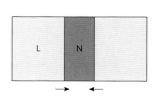

HOME SWEET HOME LAP QUILT

(See photo on page 90.)

Size: 63$\frac{1}{2}$″ × 59″

Big Blocks Needed: 2

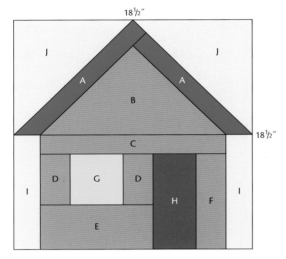

Big Block

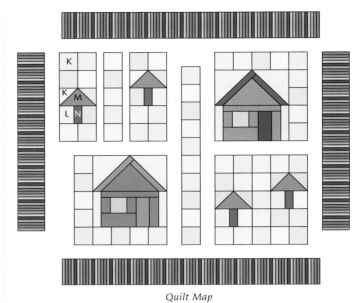

Quilt Map

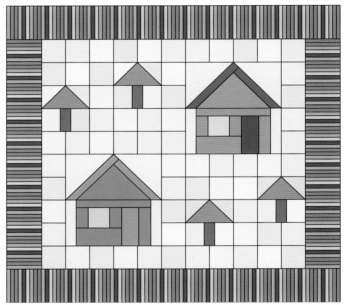

Complete Diagram

YARDAGE

ITEM	COLOR	QUANTITY NEEDED
Roof (A)		$3/8$ yard of 2 fabrics
House (B, C, D, E, F)		$3/8$ yard of 2 fabrics
Window (G)		$6'' \times 6''$ square of 2 fabrics
Door (H)		$6'' \times 10''$ rectangle of 2 fabrics
House Background (I, J)		$5/8$ yard
Background (K, L)		$3/8$ yard of 10 fabrics
Tree Top (M)		$1/4$ yard
Tree Trunk (N)		$1/8$ yard
*Borders		$1 5/8$ yards
Binding		$3/4$ yard
Backing		$70'' \times 65''$

*Based on cutting crosswise grain of the fabric. You will need to piece the border strips to get the length required.

Tree; Make 4.

Big Block; Make 2.

CUTTING

ITEM	COLOR	# TO CUT	SIZE
*A		2	$9\frac{1}{2}'' \times 11\frac{1}{2}''$
*B		1	$9\frac{1}{2}'' \times 14\frac{1}{2}''$
*C		1	$2'' \times 14\frac{1}{2}''$
*D		2	$2\frac{3}{4}'' \times 4\frac{1}{2}''$
*E		1	$4'' \times 9''$
*F		1	$2\frac{3}{4}'' \times 8''$
*G		1	$4\frac{1}{2}'' \times 4\frac{1}{2}''$
*H		1	$3\frac{3}{4}'' \times 8''$
I		4	$2\frac{1}{2}'' \times 9\frac{1}{2}''$
J		4	$9\frac{1}{2}'' \times 9\frac{1}{2}''$
**K		7	$5'' \times 5''$
**L		1	$4'' \times 5''$
M		4	$5'' \times 9\frac{1}{2}''$
N		4	$2\frac{1}{2}'' \times 5''$
Borders		7	$7\frac{1}{4}'' \times 40''$

*Cut the quantity indicated from each of the 2 fabrics.

** For K cut 7 from each of the 10 fabrics. For L cut 1 each from 8 of the fabrics.

NOTE: For sewing instructions, see page 35. Refer to the diagrams at left for the number of blocks needed.

HOME SWEET HOME QUEEN/KING QUILT

Queen: 93″× 97 1/2″

King: 97″× 101 1/2″

Big Blocks Needed: 6

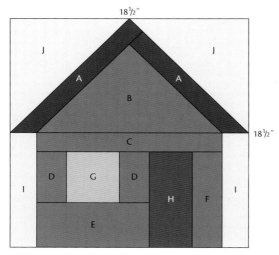

Big Block

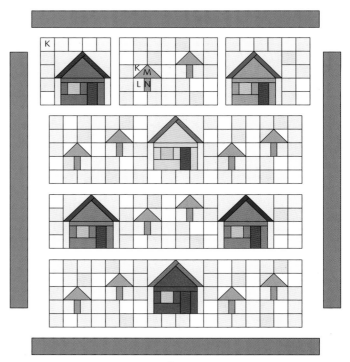

Quilt Map

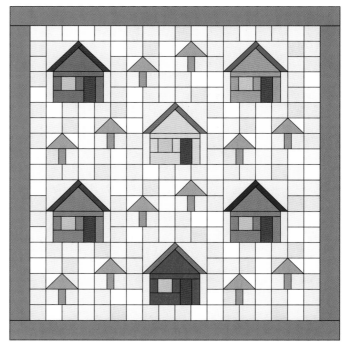

Complete Diagram

YARDAGE

ITEM	COLOR	Quantity Needed QUEEN	KING
Roof (A)		³⁄₈ yard of 6 fabrics	³⁄₈ yard of 6 fabrics
House (B, C, D, E, F)		³⁄₈ yard of 6 fabrics	³⁄₈ yard of 6 fabrics
Window (G)		6″ × 6″ square of 6 fabrics	6″ × 6″ square of 6 fabrics
Door (H)		6″ × 10″ rectangle of 6 different fabrics	6″ × 10″ rectangle of 6 different fabrics
House Background (I, J)		1¹⁄₂ yards	1¹⁄₂ yards
Background (K, L)		⁵⁄₈ yard of 12 different fabrics	⁵⁄₈ yard of 12 different fabrics
Tree Top (M)		⁵⁄₈ yard	⁵⁄₈ yard
Tree Trunk (N)		¹⁄₄ yard	¹⁄₄ yard
*Borders		2 yards	2⁵⁄₈ yards
Binding		1 yard	1¹⁄₈ yards
Backing		99″ × 104″	103″ × 108″

*Based on cutting crosswise grain of the fabric. You will need to piece the border strips to get the length required.

CUTTING for Queen and King

ITEM	COLOR	# TO CUT	SIZE
*A		2	9¹⁄₂″ × 11¹⁄₂″
*B		1	9¹⁄₂″ × 14¹⁄₂″
*C		1	2″ × 14¹⁄₂″
*D		2	2³⁄₄″ × 4¹⁄₂″
*E		1	4″ × 9″
*F		1	2³⁄₄″ × 8″
*G		1	4¹⁄₂″ × 4¹⁄₂″
*H		1	3³⁄₄″ × 8″
I		12	2¹⁄₂″ × 9¹⁄₂″
J		12	9¹⁄₂″ × 9¹⁄₂″
**K		19	5″ × 5″
**L		2	4″ × 5″
M		12	5″ × 9¹⁄₂″
N		12	2¹⁄₂″ × 5″
Queen Borders		10	6¹⁄₄″ × 40″
King Borders		10	8¹⁄₄″ × 40″

Tree; Make 12.

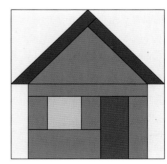

Big Block; Make 6.

*Cut the quantity indicated from each of the 6 fabrics.

**Cut the quantity indicated from each of the 12 fabrics. There will be 6 extra K squares.

NOTE: For sewing instructions, see page 35. Refer to the diagrams above for the number of blocks and units needed.

BASKETS

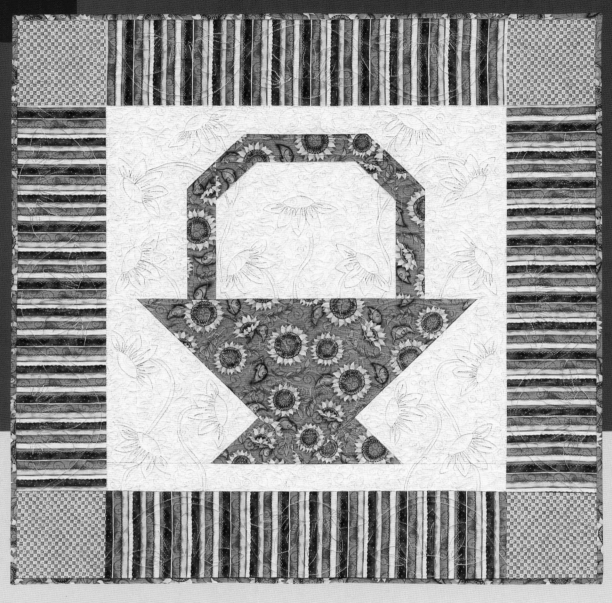

The *Really Big Basket Wallhanging* made by Nancy Johnson-Srebro.

Quilted by Veronica Nurmi.

Quilt Size: 31″ × 31″

Finished Big Block Size: 21″ × 21″

Basket blocks have long been a favorite among quilters. This one goes together quickly and you don't have to set your blocks on point. The size of this basket is perfect for showcasing those large-scale fabrics you've been hoarding.

 NO-FAIL TIPS

■ For a different look, use a dark background and a light basket fabric.

■ You can make one basket from a fat quarter if you use a different fabric for the handle.

Option A

Quilting Designs

Quilting options by Veronica Nurmi.

Option B

Note: See page 95 for stencil information.

BASKET WALLHANGING

Size: 31″ × 31″

Big Blocks Needed: 1

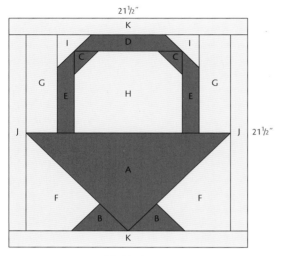

Big Block

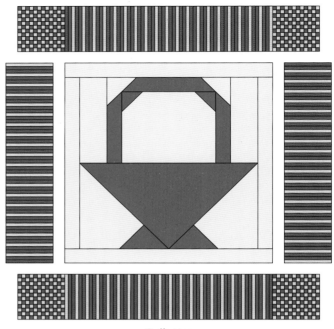

Quilt Map

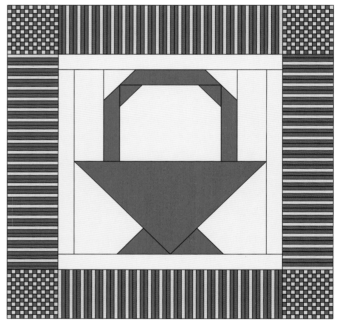

Complete Diagram

YARDAGE

ITEM	COLOR	QUANTITY NEEDED
Basket (A, B, C, D, E)	■	³/₈ yard
Background (F, G, H, I, *J, *K)	☐	³/₄ yard
Cornerstones	▦	¹/₄ yard
*Borders	▥	³/₄ yard
Binding	■	¹/₂ yard
Backing		37″ × 37″

*Based on cutting crosswise grain of the fabric.

CUTTING

ITEM	COLOR	# TO CUT	SIZE
A	■	1	9¹/₂″ × 18¹/₂″
B	■	2	5¹/₂″ × 5¹/₂″
C	■	2	2⁵/₈″ × 2⁵/₈″
D	■	1	2″ × 10″
E	■	2	2″ × 9¹/₂″
F	☐	2	9¹/₂″ × 9¹/₂″
G	☐	2	3¹/₄″ × 9¹/₂″
H	☐	1	8″ × 10″
I	☐	2	3¹/₂″ × 3¹/₂″
J	☐	2	2″ × 18¹/₂″
K	☐	2	2″ × 21¹/₂″
Cornerstones	▦	4	5¹/₄″ × 5¹/₄″
Borders	▥	4	5¹/₄″ × 21¹/₂″

NOTE: For sewing instructions, see page 44.

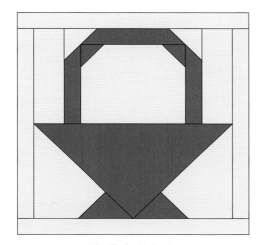

Big Block; Make 1.

Sewing the Blocks

Basket Block

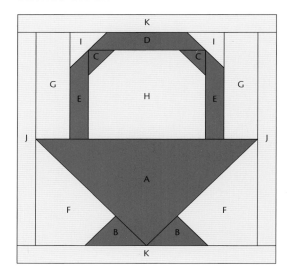

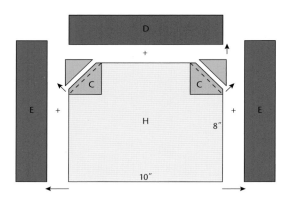

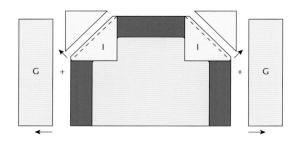

Step Three

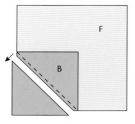

Make 2.

Step Four

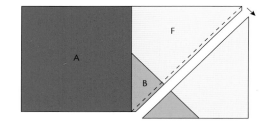

Step Five

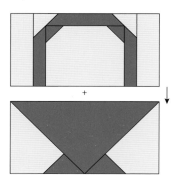

Step Six

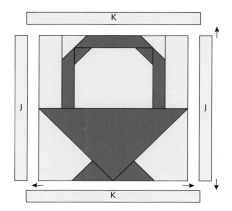

Stair Step Block (Lap, Queen/King)

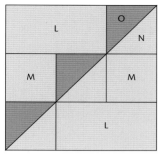

Finished Size: 21″ × 21″

Step One
On the WRONG SIDE of the light (N) square, draw a pencil line diagonally from corner to corner. Draw a line ¼″ away from the first pencil line on both sides.

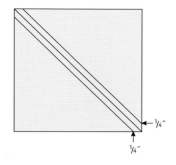

Step Two
Place the light square on top of the dark square, right sides together. Sew a couple of thread widths on the inside of the second and third pencil lines. Using a ruler and rotary cutter, cut through the first pencil line. Press toward the dark to make 2 half-square triangle blocks. Cut off the dog ears. Repeat until you have the required number of half-square triangle blocks.

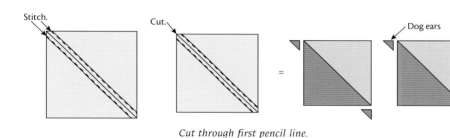

Cut through first pencil line.

Step Three

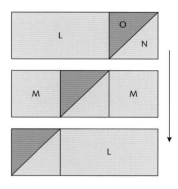

Flat Piping

Wallhanging: No piping

Lap and Queen/King: Cut 1½″-wide strips.

Sew the short ends of the strips together if needed. Press the strips in half lengthwise with wrong sides together. Trim these strips to the length and width of the quilt and follow the sewing diagrams. The piping will be ½″ wide when finished.

Step One
Align the raw edges of the piping with the sides of the quilt. Stitch, using a very scant ¼″ seam.

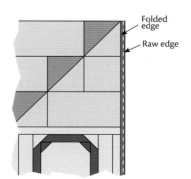

Step Two
Align the raw edges of the piping with the top/bottom edges of the quilt. Stitch.

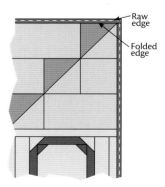

BASKET LAP QUILT
(See photo on page 91.)

Lap: 52″ × 52″

Big Blocks Needed: 2

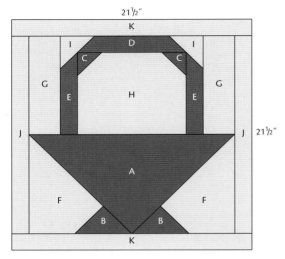

Big Block

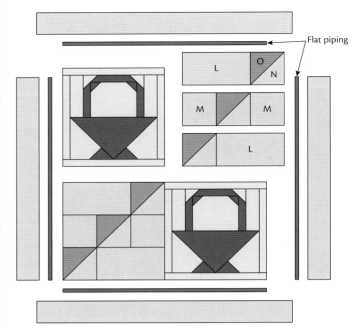

Flat piping

Quilt Map

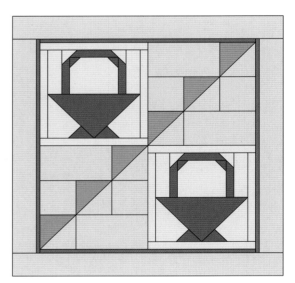

Complete Diagram

YARDAGE

ITEM	COLOR	QUANTITY NEEDED
Basket (A, B, C, D, E)		¾ yard
Background around the basket (F, G, H, I, *J, *K)		1⅛ yards
Background for the Stair Step Block (*L, M, N) and *Borders		1¾ yards
Stair Step Block (O)		⅜ yard
*Flat Piping		⅜ yard
Binding		⅝ yard
Backing		58″ × 58″

*Based on cutting crosswise grain of the fabric. You will need to piece the flat piping and border strips to get the length required.

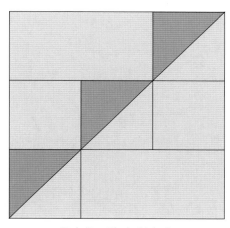

Stair Step Block; Make 2.

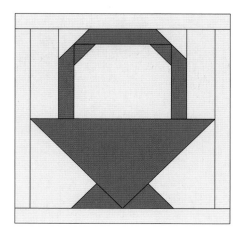

Big Block; Make 2.

CUTTING

ITEM	COLOR	# TO CUT	SIZE
A		2	9½″ × 18½″
B		4	5½″ × 5½″
C		4	2⅝″ × 2⅝″
D		2	2″ × 10″
E		4	2″ × 9½″
F		4	9½″ × 9½″
G		4	3¼″ × 9½″
H		2	8″ × 10″
I		4	3½″ × 3½″
J		4	2″ × 18½″
K		4	2″ × 21½″
L		4	7½″ × 14½″
M		4	7½″ × 7½″
N		3	7⅞″ × 7⅞″
O		3	7⅞″ × 7⅞″
Flat Piping		5	1½″ × 40″
Borders		5	5¼″ × 40″

NOTE: For sewing instructions, see pages 44–45. Refer to the diagrams at left for the number of units and blocks needed.

BASKET QUEEN/KING QUILT

Queen Size: 94″ × 94″

King Size: 104″ × 104″

Big Blocks Needed: 8

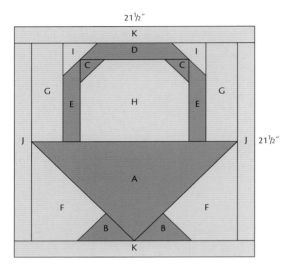

Big Block

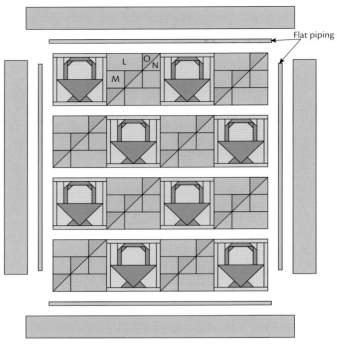

Quilt Map

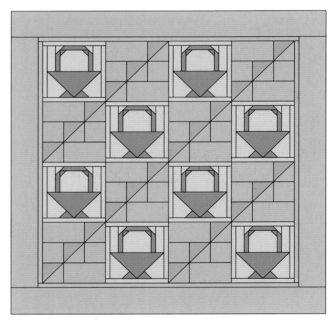

Complete Diagram

YARDAGE

ITEM	COLOR	QUANTITY NEEDED QUEEN	KING
Basket (A, B, C, D, E)	■	2¼ yards	2¼ yards
Background for the basket (F, G, H, I, *J, *K)	□	3¾ yards	3¾ yards
Background for the Stair Step Block (*L, M, N) and *Borders	□	5¼ yards	7 yards
Stair Step Block (O)	■	1 yard	1 yard
*Flat Piping	■	½ yard	½ yard
Binding	■	1 yard	1⅛ yards
Backing		100″ x 100″	110″ x 110″

*Based on cutting crosswise grain of the fabric. You will need to piece the flat piping and border strips to get the length required.

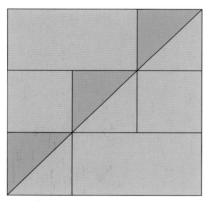

Stair Step Block; Make 8.

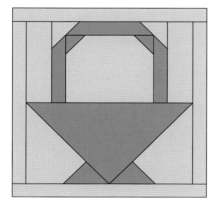

Big Block; Make 8.

CUTTING for Queen and King

ITEM	COLOR	# TO CUT	SIZE
A	■	8	9½″ × 18½″
B	■	16	5½″ × 5½″
C	■	16	2⅝″ × 2⅝″
D	■	8	2″ × 10″
E	■	16	2″ × 9½″
F	□	16	9½″ × 9½″
G	□	16	3¼″ × 9½″
H	□	8	8″ × 10″
I	□	16	3½″ × 3½″
J	□	16	2″ × 18½″
K	□	16	2″ × 21½″
L	□	16	7½″ × 14½″
M	□	16	7½″ × 7½″
N	□	12	7⅞″ × 7⅞″
O	■	12	7⅞″ × 7⅞″
Flat Piping	□	9	1½″ × 40″
Queen Borders	□	10	5¼″ × 40″
King Borders	□	11	10¼″ × 40″

NOTE: For sewing instructions, see pages 44–45. Refer to the diagrams at left for the number of blocks needed.

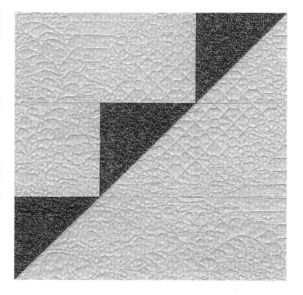

KAISER'S PATH

Kaiser's Path Wallhanging made by Nancy Johnson-Srebro.

Quilted by Veronica Nurmi.

Quilt Size: $36\frac{1}{2}'' \times 36\frac{1}{2}''$

Finished Big Block Size: $18'' \times 18''$

Finished Quarter-Block Size: $9'' \times 9''$

Strip piecing and working with quarter-blocks has never been easier! Plus you get a "free" Bonus Block from this method. There are so many ways to arrange the quarter-blocks that you'll be creating your own spectacular designs right from the start.

 NO-FAIL TIPS

■ This block is so versatile that you can create end-less variations by experimenting with the placement of the lights, mediums, and darks. Or try jewel tones, Amish colors, or 30s fabrics for a unique look. For a bold graphic look use black, white, gray, and an accent color such as red or hot pink.

■ Have fun rearranging the blocks to see what new combinations you can come up with. Try setting the blocks on point, adding sashing, or arranging them in a strippy setting.

Option A

Quilting Designs

Quilting options by Veronica Nurmi.

Option B

KAISER'S PATH WALLHANGING

Size: $36^1/2''$ x $36^1/2''$

Big Blocks Needed: 8 quarter-blocks

Bonus Blocks Needed: 8 quarter-blocks

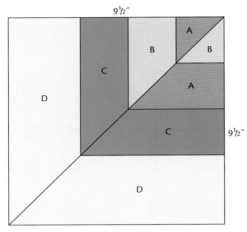

Quarter of Big Block

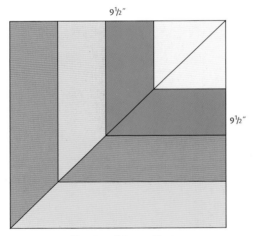

Quarter of Bonus Block

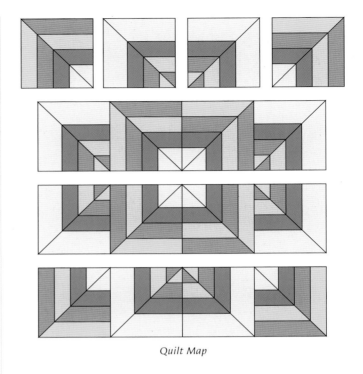

Quilt Map

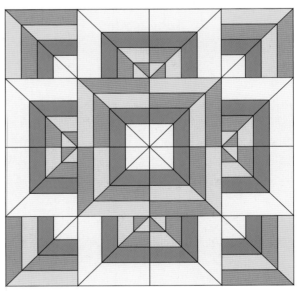

Complete Diagram

YARDAGE

ITEM	COLOR	QUANTITY NEEDED
*A		⅜ yard
*B		⅜ yard
*C		⅜ yard
*D		⅝ yard
Binding		½ yard
Backing		42″ × 42″

*Based on cutting crosswise grain of the fabric.

CUTTING

ITEM	COLOR	# TO CUT	SIZE
A		4	2½″ × 40″
B		4	2½″ × 40″
C		4	2½″ × 40″
D		4	3⅞″ × 40″

NOTE: For sewing instructions, see pages 53–55. Refer to the diagrams below for the number of quarter-blocks needed.

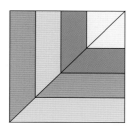

Quarter of Big Block (Kaiser's Path); Make 8.

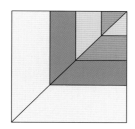

Quarter of Bonus Block (Kaiser's Bonus); Make 8.

After sewing 8 quarter-blocks of Kaiser's Path, you will automatically have 8 quarter-blocks of Kaiser's Bonus Block.

Sewing the Quarter-Blocks

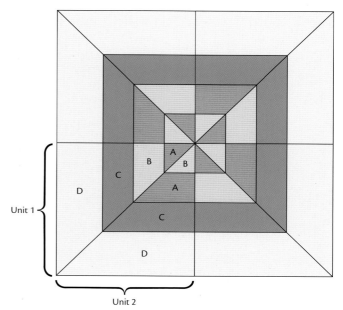

Kaiser's Path Big Block

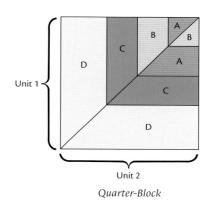

Quarter-Block

Step One
Unit 1

Sew A, B, C, and D strips together as shown. Make 2 strip sets for either the wallhanging or the lap quilt. Cut each set into 4 sections, 9⅞" × 9⅞", for a total of 8. (For the Queen/King quilt, make 12 strip sets and cut a total of 48 sections, 9⅞" × 9⅞".)

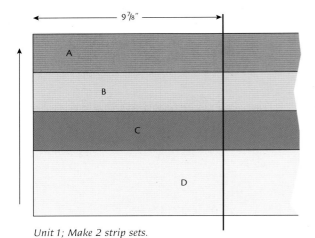

Unit 1; Make 2 strip sets.

Step Two
Unit 2

Sew A, B, C, and D strips together, reversing the order of the A and B strips. Make 2 strip sets for either the wallhanging or the lap quilt. Cut each set into 4 sections, 9⅞" × 9⅞", for a total of 8. (For the Queen/King quilt, make 12 strip sets and cut a total of 48 sections, 9⅞" × 9⅞".)

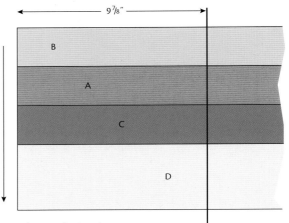

Unit 2; Make 2 strip sets.

Step Three

On the WRONG SIDE of Unit 1, draw a pencil line diagonally from corner to corner. Draw a line ¼" away on both sides of the first pencil line.

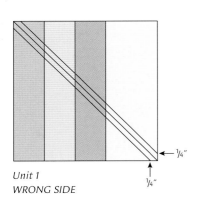

Unit 1
WRONG SIDE

Step Four

Place Unit 1 on top of Unit 2, right sides together. Align and pin the seams to keep them together.

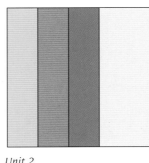

Unit 2
RIGHT SIDE up

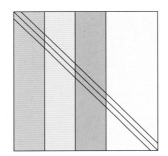

Unit 1
Place Unit 1, WRONG SIDE up, on top of Unit 2.

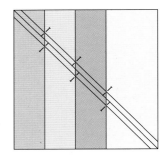

Align and pin the seams.

Step Five

Sew a couple of thread widths on the inside of the second and third pencil lines. Using a ruler and rotary cutter, cut through the first pencil line. Press and cut off the dog ears. This will make one quarter of the Kaiser's Path block and one quarter of Kaiser's Bonus.

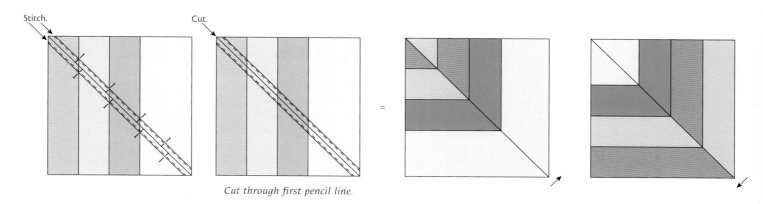

Cut through first pencil line.

BLOCK ASSEMBLY

Quarter-blocks are used for the wallhanging and lap quilt. Full blocks are used for the Queen and King quilts.

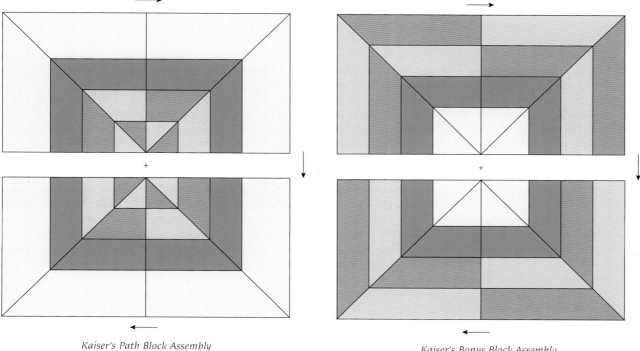

Kaiser's Path Block Assembly

Kaiser's Bonus Block Assembly

KAISER'S PATH LAP QUILT

(See the photo on page 92.)

Size: 48″ × 48″

Big Blocks Needed: 8 quarter-blocks

Bonus Blocks Needed: 8 quarter-blocks

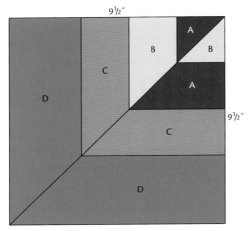

Quarter of Big Block

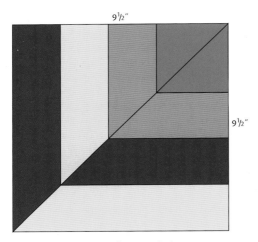

Quarter of Bonus Block

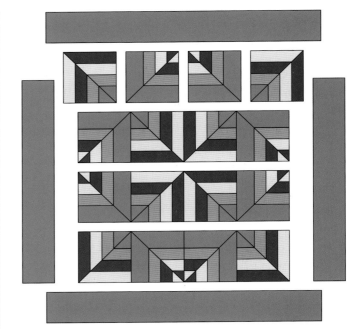

Quilt Map

Complete Diagram

YARDAGE

ITEM	COLOR	QUANTITY NEEDED
*A	■	3/8 yard
*B	□	3/8 yard
*C	■	3/8 yard
*D, *Borders	■	1 1/2 yards
Binding	■	5/8 yard
Backing		54″ × 54″

*Based on cutting crosswise grain of the fabric. You will need to piece the top and bottom border strips to get the length required.

CUTTING

ITEM	COLOR	# TO CUT	SIZE
A	■	4	2 1/2″ × 40″
B	□	4	2 1/2″ × 40″
C	■	4	2 1/2″ × 40″
D	■	4	3 7/8″ × 40″
Borders	■	5	6 1/4″ × 40″

NOTE: For sewing instructions, see pages 53–55. Refer to the diagrams at left for the number of quarter-blocks needed.

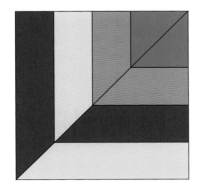

Quarter of Big Block (Kaiser's Path); Make 8.

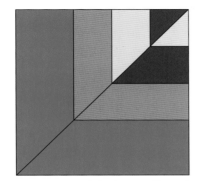

Quarter of Bonus Block (Kaiser's Bonus); Make 8.

After sewing 8 quarter-blocks of Kaiser's Path, you will automatically have 8 quarter-blocks of Kaiser's Bonus.

KAISER'S PATH QUEEN/KING QUILT

Queen: 100″ × 100″

King: 106″ × 106″

Big Blocks Needed: 12

Bonus Blocks Needed: 12

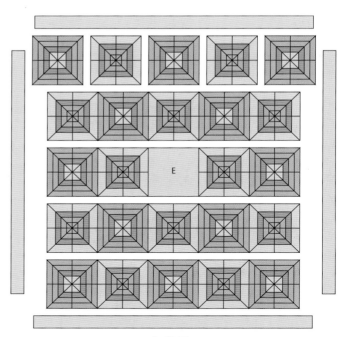

Quilt Map

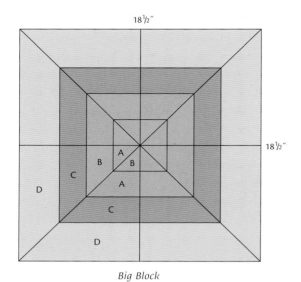

Big Block

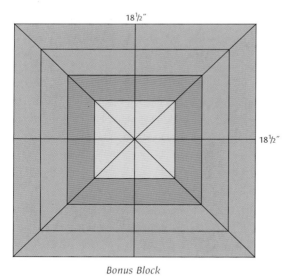

Bonus Block

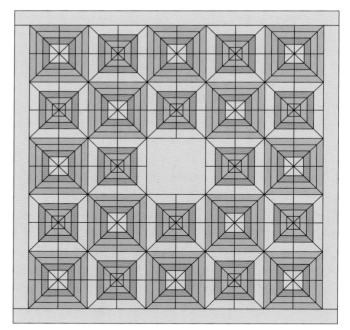

Complete Diagram

YARDAGE

ITEM	COLOR	QUEEN	KING
*A		1⅞ yards	1⅞ yards
*B		1⅞ yards	1⅞ yards
*C		1⅞ yards	1⅞ yards
*D, E, *Borders		4⅞ yards	6 yards
Binding		1 yard	1⅛ yards
Backing		106″ × 106″	112″ × 112″

*Based on cutting crosswise grain of the fabric. You will need to piece the borders to get the length required.

CUTTING

ITEM COLOR		# TO CUT	SIZE
A		24	2½″ × 40″
B		24	2½″ × 40″
C		24	2½″ × 40″
D		24	3⅞″ × 40″
E		1	18½″ × 18½″
Queen Borders		10	5¼″ × 40″
King Borders		11	8¼″ × 40″

NOTE: For sewing instructions, see pages 53–55. Refer to the diagrams at left for the number of blocks needed.

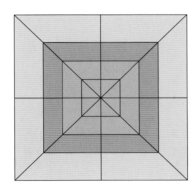

Big Block; Make 12.

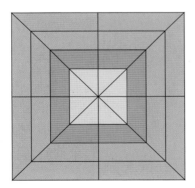

Bonus Block; Make 12.

CAROLINA LILY

Carolina Lily Wallhanging made by Nancy Johnson-Srebro.

Quilted by Cindy Needham.

Quilt Size: $33^{1}/_{2}$″ × $37^{1}/_{2}$″

Finished Big Block Size: 20″ × 24″

Finished Pinwheel Size: 4″ × 4″

I've always loved this classic block. It's quick and easy to sew with only squares and rectangles. Add a few pinwheels and watch this wallhanging dance!

 ## NO-FAIL TIP

For the wallhanging I used 2 different colors for the lily petals and repeated 1 of those colors for the pinwheels. When I decided to use scraps for the queen-size quilt (page 93), I used my "controlled color" theory. This means I chose 4-5 colors for the petals and used different shades of those colors throughout the petals and pinwheels. This guaranteed that the quilt would have a scrappy look and that the colors would be pleasing together.

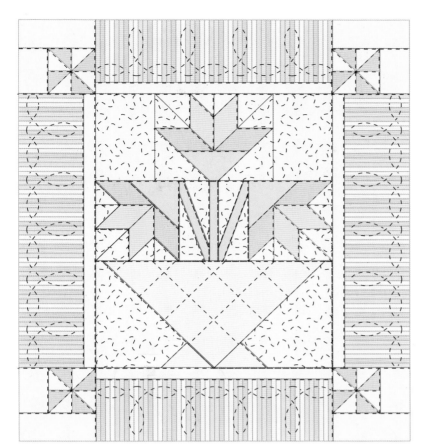

Option A

Quilting Designs

Quilting options by Cindy Needham.

Note: See page 95 for stencil information.

Option B

Carolina Lily Wallhanging

Size: $33^{1}/_{2}'' \times 37^{1}/_{2}''$

Big Blocks Needed: 1

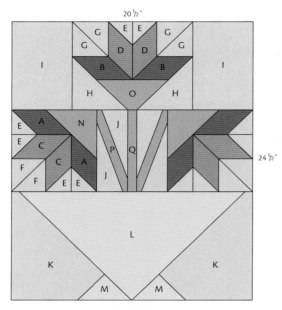

Big Block

Quilt Map

Complete Diagram

YARDAGE

ITEM	COLOR	QUANTITY NEEDED
Petals (A, B), Pinwheels (R)	■	1/4 yard
Petals (C, D)	■	1/4 yard
Background (E, F, G, H, I, J, K)	□	1 1/4 yards
Pinwheels (S, T, U)		
*Inner Border (V, W)		
Basket (L, M)	□	3/8 yard
Stems (N, O, P, Q)	■	1/4 yard
*Outer Borders (X, Y)	▥	7/8 yard
Binding	■	1/2 yard
Backing		40″ × 44″

*Based on cutting crosswise grain of the fabric.

CUTTING

ITEM	COLOR	# TO CUT	SIZE
A	■	4	2 1/2″ × 7 1/2″
B	■	2	2 1/2″ × 5 1/2″
C	■	4	2 1/2″ × 7 1/2″
D	■	2	2 1/2″ 5 1/2″
E	□	10	2 1/2″ × 2 1/2″
F	□	4	3 1/2″ × 7 1/2″
G	□	4	3 1/2″ × 5 1/2″
H	□	2	5 1/8″ × 5 1/8″
I	□	2	5 1/2″ × 8 1/8″
J	□	4	3 1/8″ × 6 1/2″
K	□	2	9 7/8″ × 10 1/2″
L	□	1	9 7/8″ × 19 1/4″
M	□	2	5″ × 5″
N	■	2	4 1/2″ × 4 1/2″
O	■	1	3 1/8″ × 10 1/2″
P	■	2	3 1/8″ × 7 1/2″
Q	■	1	1 1/4″ × 7 1/2″
R	■	8	2 7/8″ × 2 7/8″
S	□	8	2 7/8″ × 2 7/8″
T	□	4	3″ × 4 1/2″
U	□	4	3″ × 7″
V	□	2	1 1/2″ × 20 1/2″
W	□	2	1 1/2″ × 24 1/2″
X	▥	2	6″ × 24 1/2″
Y	▥	2	6″ × 20 1/2″

NOTE: For sewing instructions, see pages 64–67. Refer to the diagrams at left for the number of blocks and units needed.

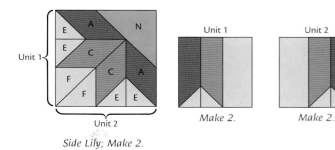

Side Lily; Make 2.

Unit 1 — *Make 2.*

Unit 2 — *Make 2.*

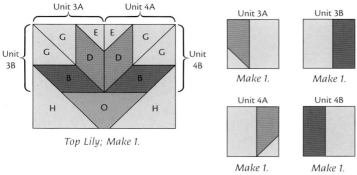

Top Lily; Make 1.

Unit 3A — *Make 1.*

Unit 3B — *Make 1.*

Unit 4A — *Make 1.*

Unit 4B — *Make 1.*

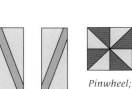

Left Stem; Make 1.

Right Stem; Make 1.

Pinwheel; Make 4.

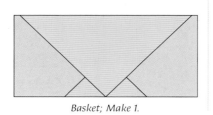

Basket; Make 1.

Sewing the Blocks and Units

SIDE LILY

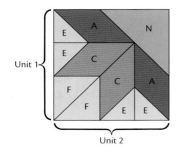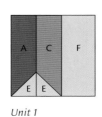

Unit 1

Unit 2

Step One

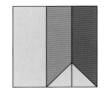

Unit 1

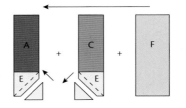

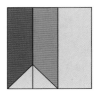

Unit 1; Make 2.

Step Two

Unit 2

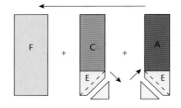

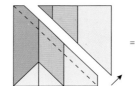

Unit 2; Make 2.

Step Three

Draw a diagonal line on the WRONG SIDE of all Unit 2s, as shown. Place Unit 2, WRONG SIDE up, on top of Unit 1. Align, sew, press, and trim.

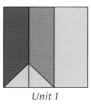

Unit 1
RIGHT SIDE up

Pencil line

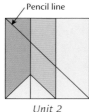

Unit 2
WRONG SIDE up

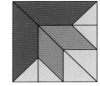

=

Step Four

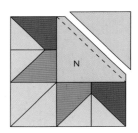

Make 2.

TOP LILY—LEFT HALF

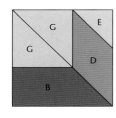

Step One

Unit 3A

+

Step Two

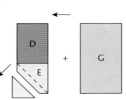

Unit 3B

+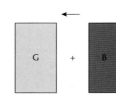

Step Three

Draw a diagonal line on the WRONG SIDE of Unit 3B, as shown. Place Unit 3B, WRONG SIDE up, on top of Unit 3A. Align, sew, press, and trim.

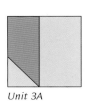

Unit 3A
RIGHT SIDE up

Pencil line

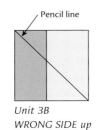

Unit 3B
WRONG SIDE up

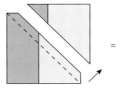

Make 1.

TOP LILY—RIGHT HALF

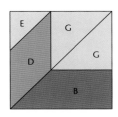

Step One

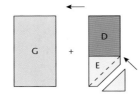

Unit 4A

Step Two

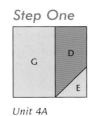

Unit 4B

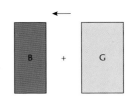

Step Three

Draw a diagonal line on the WRONG SIDE of Unit 4A, as shown. Place Unit 4A, WRONG SIDE up, on top of Unit 4B. Align, sew, press, and trim.

Unit 4B
RIGHT SIDE up

Pencil line

Unit 4A
WRONG SIDE up

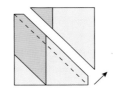

Make 1.

TOP LILY ASSEMBLY

Step One

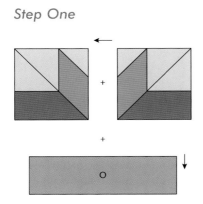

Step Two

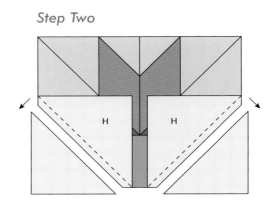

LEFT STEM

Step One

Place pencil marks on one P and two J pieces, as shown. Draw a pencil line on the WRONG SIDE of J from the ¼" mark to the lower corner of the rectangle.

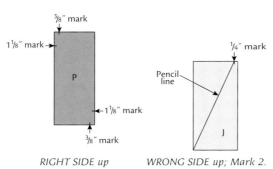

3⁄8" mark

1⅛" mark→

¼" mark

Pencil line

←1⅛" mark

3⁄8" mark

P

J

RIGHT SIDE up   *WRONG SIDE up; Mark 2.*

Step Two

Place the diagonal pencil line of one J over the left 1⅛" mark on P. J will overhang P slightly.

Align the ¼" mark on J with the bottom 3⁄8" mark on P. Sew just to the left of the pencil line.

Press but don't trim the seam allowance yet.

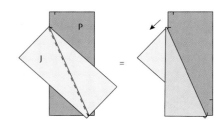

P

J

=

Step Three

Align the ¼" mark on the second J with the top 3⁄8" mark on P.

Place the diagonal pencil line over the right 1⅛" mark on P. J will overhang P slightly. Sew just to the right of the pencil line.

Press but don't trim the seam allowance yet.

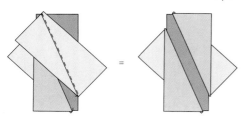

=

Step Four

With the WRONG SIDE up, trim the edges even with P.

Trim the two seam allowances ¼" from the stitching line.

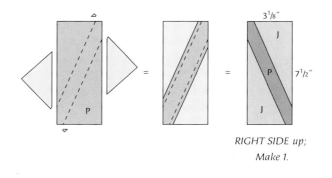

P

=

=

3⅛"

J

P

J

7½"

RIGHT SIDE up;
Make 1.

RIGHT STEM

Step One

Place pencil marks on one P and two J pieces, as shown. Draw a pencil line on the WRONG SIDE of J from the ¼" mark to the lower corner of the rectangle.

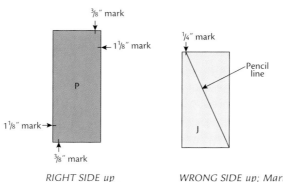

3⁄8" mark

←1⅛" mark

¼" mark

Pencil line

P

1⅛" mark→

J

3⁄8" mark

RIGHT SIDE up   *WRONG SIDE up; Mark 2.*

Step Two

Place the diagonal pencil line of J over the right 1⅛" mark on P. J will overhang P slightly.

Align the ¼" mark on J with the bottom 3⁄8" mark on P. Sew just to the right of the pencil line.

Press but don't trim the seam allowance yet.

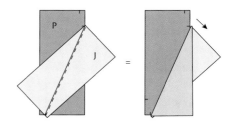

P

J

=

Step Three

Align the ¼" mark on J with the top ⅜" mark on P.

Place the diagonal pencil line over the left 1⅛" mark on P. J will overhang P slightly. Sew just to the left of the pencil line.

Press but don't trim the seam allowance yet.

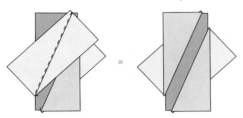

Step Four

With the WRONG SIDE up, trim the edges even with P.

Then, trim the two seam allowances ¼" from the stitching line.

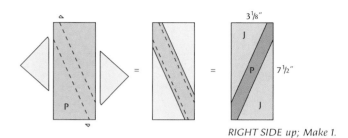

RIGHT SIDE up; Make 1.

BASKET

Step One

Step Two

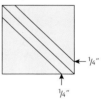

BIG BLOCK ASSEMBLY

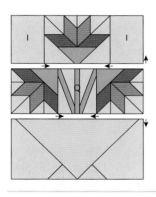

PINWHEELS

Finished sizes:

Wallhanging 4" × 4"

Lap 7" × 7"

Queen and King 10" × 10"

Note that the position of R and S are reversed for the lap, queen, and king size quilts.

Step One

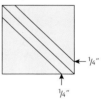

On the WRONG SIDE of the light (S) square, draw a pencil line diagonally from corner to corner. Draw a line ¼" away from the first pencil line on both sides.

Step Two

Place the marked light (S) square on top of the dark (R) square, right sides together. Sew a couple of thread widths on the inside of the second and third pencil lines. Using a ruler and rotary cutter, cut through the first pencil line to yield 2 pieced squares.

Press toward the dark to make 2 half-square triangle blocks. Cut off the dog ears. Repeat until you have the required number of half-square triangle blocks.

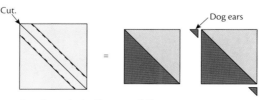

Cut through the first pencil line.

Step Three

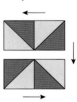

Carolina Lily Lap Quilt

Lap: 52″ × 59″

Big Blocks Needed: 1

Big Block

Quilt Map

Complete Diagram

YARDAGE

ITEM	COLOR	QUANTITY NEEDED
Petals (A, B)		1/4 yard
Petals (C, D)		1/4 yard
Background (E, F, G, H, I, J, K)		3 3/8 yards
Pinwheels (S)		
*Inner Borders (T, U)		
*Outer Borders		
Basket (L, M)		3/8 yard
Stems (N, O, P, Q)		1/4 yard
Pinwheels (R)		3/8 yard of 4 different fabrics
Binding		5/8 yard
Backing		58″ × 65″

*Based on cutting crosswise grain of the fabric. You will need to piece the borders to get the length required.

CUTTING

ITEM	COLOR	# TO CUT	SIZE
A		4	2 1/2″ × 7 1/2″
B		2	2 1/2″ × 5 1/2″
C		4	2 1/2″ × 7 1/2″
D		2	2 1/2″ × 5 1/2″
E		10	2 1/2″ × 2 1/2″
F		4	3 1/2″ × 7 1/2″
G		4	3 1/2″ × 5 1/2″
H		2	5 1/8″ × 5 1/8″
I		2	5 1/2″ × 8 1/8″
J		4	3 1/8″ × 6 1/2″
K		2	9 7/8″ × 10 1/2″
L		1	9 7/8″ × 19 1/4″
M		2	5″ × 5″
N		2	4 1/2″ × 4 1/2″
O		1	3 1/8″ × 10 1/2″
P		2	3 1/8″ × 7 1/2″
Q		1	1 1/4″ × 7 1/2″
*R		12	4 3/8″ × 4 3/8″
S		44	4 3/8″ × 4 3/8″
T		2	4 1/2″ × 35 1/2″
U		2	6″ × 20 1/2″
Borders		6	5 1/4″ × 40″

*Cut from each of the 4 fabrics.

NOTE: For sewing instructions, see pages 64–67. Refer to the diagrams at left for the number of blocks and units needed.

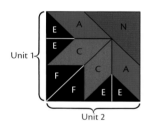

Side Lily; Make 2.

Unit 1

Make 2.

Unit 2

Make 2.

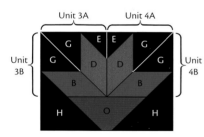

Top Lily; Make 1.

Unit 3A — *Make 1.*

Unit 3B — *Make 1.*

Unit 4A — *Make 1.*

Unit 4B — *Make 1.*

Left Stem; Make 1.

Right Stem; Make 1.

Pinwheel; Make 22.

Basket; Make 1.

Carolina Lily Queen/King Quilt

(See photo on page 93.)

Queen: 94″ × 104″

King: 100″ × 110″

Big Blocks Needed: 4

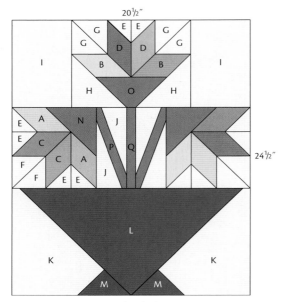

Big Block

Complete Diagram

Quilt Map

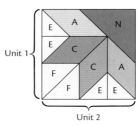

Side Lily; Make 8.

Unit 1 Make 8.

Unit 2 Make 8.

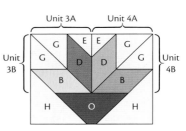

Top Lily; Make 4.

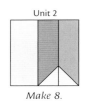

Unit 3A Make 4.

Unit 3B Make 4.

Unit 4A Make 4.

Unit 4B Make 4.

Left Stem; Make 4.

Right Stem; Make 4.

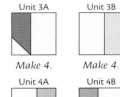

Pinwheel; Make 26.

Basket; Make 4.

YARDAGE

ITEM	COLOR	QUEEN	KING
		Quantity Needed	
Petals (A, B, C, D)		$^1/_8$ yard of 8 different fabrics or scraps	$^1/_8$ yard of 8 different fabrics or scraps
Background (E, F, G, H, I, J, K)		9$^1/_2$ yards	11 yards
Pinwheels (S)			
*Inner Borders (T, U, V)			
*Outer Borders			
Basket (L, M)		$^3/_8$ yard of 4 different fabrics	$^3/_8$ yard of 4 different fabrics
Stems (N, O, P, Q)		$^5/_8$ yard	$^5/_8$ yard
Pinwheels (R)		$^5/_8$ yard of 4 different fabrics	$^5/_8$ yard of 4 different fabrics
Binding		1$^1/_8$ yards	1$^1/_4$ yards
Backing		100″ × 110″	106″ × 116″

*Based on cutting crosswise grain of the fabric. You will need to piece T, U, and the outer borders to get the length required.

CUTTING for Queen and King

ITEM	COLOR	# TO CUT	SIZE
*A		16	2$^1/_2$″ × 7$^1/_2$″
*B		8	2$^1/_2$″ × 5$^1/_2$″
*C		16	2$^1/_2$″ × 7$^1/_2$″
*D		8	2$^1/_2$″ × 5$^1/_2$″
E		40	2$^1/_2$″ × 2$^1/_2$″
F		16	3$^1/_2$″ × 7$^1/_2$″
G		16	3$^1/_2$″ × 5$^1/_2$″
H		8	5$^1/_8$″ × 5$^1/_8$″
I		8	5$^1/_2$″ × 8$^1/_8$″
J		16	3$^1/_8$″ × 6$^1/_2$″
K		8	9$^7/_8$″ × 10$^1/_2$″
**L		1	9$^7/_8$″ × 19$^1/_4$″
**M		2	5″ × 5″
N		8	4$^1/_2$″ × 4$^1/_2$″

ITEM	COLOR	# TO CUT	SIZE
O		4	3$^1/_8$″ × 10$^1/_2$″
P		8	3$^1/_8$″ × 7$^1/_2$″
Q		4	1$^1/_4$″ × 7$^1/_2$″
**R		14	5$^7/_8$″ × 5$^7/_8$″
S		52	5$^7/_8$″ × 5$^7/_8$″
T		4	3$^7/_8$″ × 30$^1/_2$″
U		2	3$^3/_4$″ × 30$^1/_2$″
V		6	4$^1/_2$″ × 20$^1/_2$″
Queen Borders		10	12$^1/_4$″ × 40″
King Borders		12	15$^1/_4$″ × 40″

*Cut from various scraps.

**Cut from each of the 4 fabrics.

NOTE: For sewing instructions, see pages 64–67. Refer to the diagrams on page 70 for the number of blocks and units needed.

TREE OF LIFE

Tree of Life Wallhanging made by Nancy Johnson-Srebro.

Quilted by Veronica Nurmi.

Quilt Size: 35″ × 35″

Finished Big Block Size: 29$\frac{1}{2}$″ × 29$\frac{1}{2}$″

Finished Tree Block Size: 20″ × 20″

I've been enchanted with the Tree of Life block for years but never made one because I couldn't face working with the bias edges of all those diamonds. Now you don't have to worry about that problem because my Diamond-Free method uses only squares and rectangles. For the tree leaves all you have to cut are 3 different size rectangles!

 NO-FAIL TIP

At first I thought the more colors and fabrics I used, the better the block would look. After doing several mock-ups (page 79), I discovered that the blocks looked better if I limited myself to 12-14 fabrics, and chose slightly different shades of some of those colors. For example, in one block I used several shades of green, red, and brown. For some pizzazz I added two shades of orange and 1 shade of yellow.

Option A

Quilting Designs

Quilting options by Veronica Nurmi.

Note: See page 95 for stencil information.

Option B

TREE OF LIFE WALLHANGING

Size: 35″ × 35″

Big Blocks Needed: 1

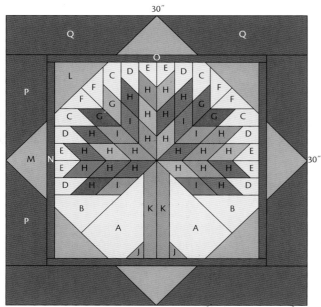

G LT GR 1 Big Block   (2¼ × 8¼)
   RED -2   PURPLE 1

H Lt Gr. 2
   BROWN 4/5
   PINK 4   (2¼ × 4¾)
   DK GREEN 4
   DKER "   1
   PURPLE 5
   TURQ 3

I PURP -2
   GR. 2
   DK G. 1 2¼ × 6½
   BLUE 1

J TREE TRUNK

   "

K

Quilt Map

Complete Diagram

YARDAGE

ITEM	COLOR	QUANTITY NEEDED
Background (A,B,C,D,E,F)	☐	1 1/8 yards
Leaves (G, H, I)	▥	1/8 yard each of 12-14 different fabrics
Trunk (J, *K)	▨	1/8 yard
Triangles (L, M)	▨	3/4 yard
*Outer Borders		
Inner Borders (N,O,P, Q)	▨	7/8 yard
Binding	▨	1/2 yard
Backing		41" × 41"

*Based on cutting crosswise grain of the fabric.

CUTTING

ITEM	COLOR	# TO CUT	SIZE
A	☐	2	9 1/4" × 10 1/2"
B	☐	2	7" × 10 1/2"
C	☐	4	2 1/4" × 4 1/2"
D	☐	6	2 1/4" × 3 3/4"
E	☐	6	2 1/4" × 3"
F	☐	4	5 1/4" × 10 1/2"
G	▥	4	2 1/4" × 8 1/4"
H	▥	24	2 1/4" × 4 3/4"
I	▥	6	2 1/4" × 6 1/2"
J	▨	2	2 1/4" × 2 1/4"
K	▨	2	1 3/4" × 10 1/2"
L	▨	4	5 3/4" × 5 3/4"
M	▨	4	4 1/2" × 8 1/2"
N	▨	2	1 1/4" × 20 1/2"
O	▨	2	1 1/4" × 22"
P	▨	4	4 1/2" × 11 1/4"
Q	▨	4	4 1/2" × 15 1/4"
Side Borders	☐	2	3" × 30"
Top/Bottom Borders	▨	2	3" × 35"

NOTE: For sewing instructions, see pages 76–79. Refer to the diagrams at left and below for the number of blocks and units needed.

Unit 1; Make 2.

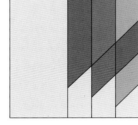

Unit 2; Make 2.

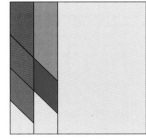

Unit 3A; Make 1.

Unit 3B; Make 1.

Unit 4A; Make 1.

Unit 4B; Make 1.

Side Units; Make 2.

Top and Bottom Units; Make 2.

Big Block; Make 1.

Sewing the Blocks and Units

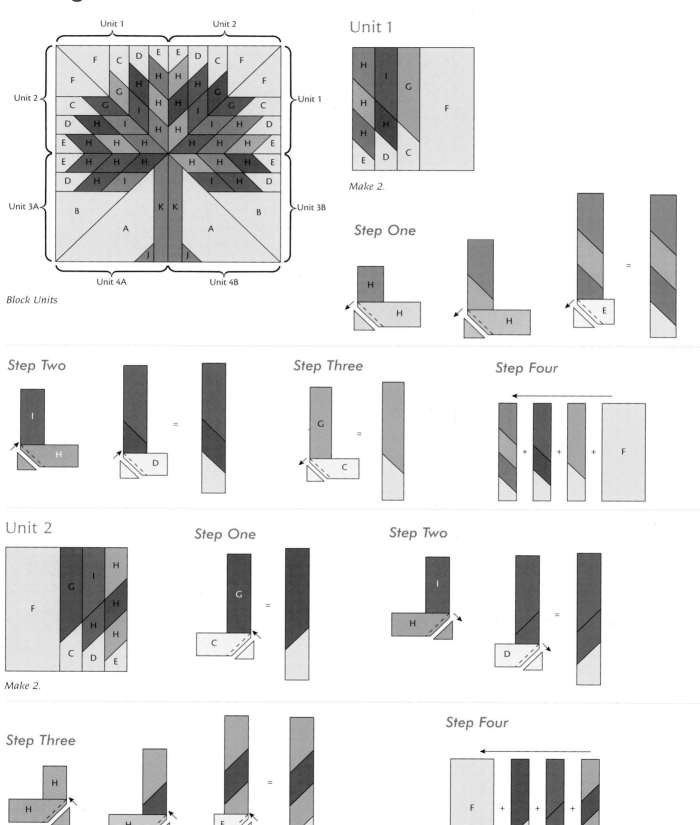

Block Units

Unit 1

Make 2.

Step One

Step Two

Step Three

Step Four

Unit 2

Make 2.

Step One

Step Two

Step Three

Step Four

Unit 3A

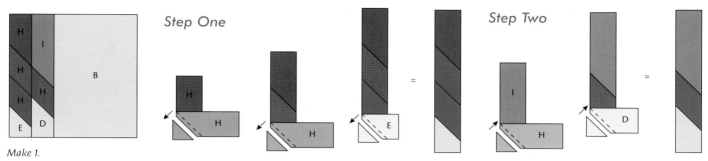

Make 1.

Step One

Step Two

Step Three

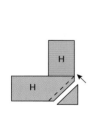

Unit 3B

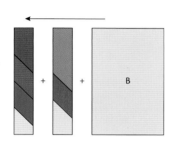

Make 1.

Step One

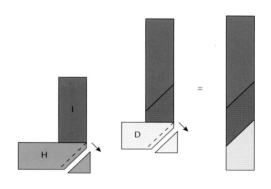

Step Two

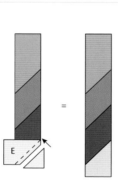

Step Three

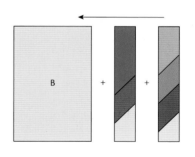

Units 4A and 4B

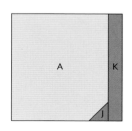
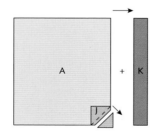

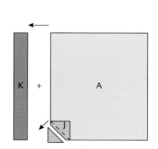

Unit 4A; Make 1.

Unit 4B; Make 1

BIG BLOCK ASSEMBLY

Step One

Draw a diagonal line on the WRONG SIDE of all Unit 2s, as shown. Place Unit 2, WRONG SIDE up, on top of Unit 1. Align, sew, and press. Trim ¼" from the sewing line. Make 2 for each block.

Unit 1; RIGHT SIDE up

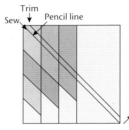

Unit 2; WRONG SIDE up

Step Two

Draw a diagonal line on the WRONG SIDE of Unit 4A, as shown. Place Unit 4A, WRONG SIDE up, on top of Unit 3A. Align, sew, press, and trim.

Unit 3A; RIGHT SIDE up

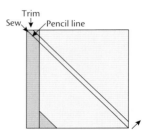

Unit 4A; WRONG SIDE up

Step Three

Draw a diagonal line on the WRONG SIDE of Unit 3B, as shown. Place Unit 3B, WRONG SIDE up, on top of Unit 4B. Align, sew, and press. Trim ¼" from the sewing line.

Unit 4B; RIGHT SIDE up

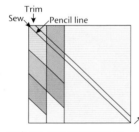

Unit 3B; WRONG SIDE up

Step Four

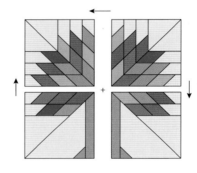

Step Five

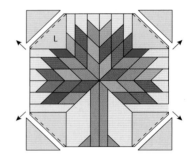

BLOCK BORDERS

Step One

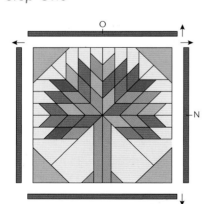

Step Two

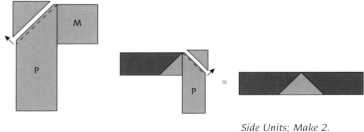

Side Units; Make 2.

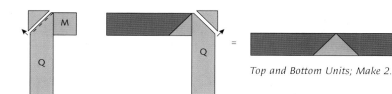

Top and Bottom Units; Make 2.

Color Placement for the Leaves

I found that the easiest way to get the colors where I wanted them was to do a mock-up of the block. First I cut three or four $1^3/4'' \times 4^1/4''$ rectangles of each color, and drew two 45° diagonal lines as shown. Then I cut off the corners of the rectangle to form the diamond shape.

 =

I place the diamond shapes on a piece of batting to create the leaves of the tree.

Once I am satisfied with the arrangement, I start cutting out rectangles for the block. To keep the background and leaf colors in the correct position I place each rectangle on a spare cutting mat to match the mock-up and the Tree Block Diagram on page 76.

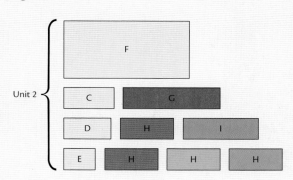

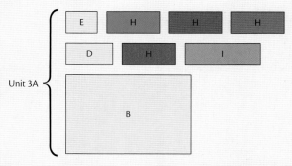

Then I carry the cutting mat to my sewing machine and keep the pieces in the proper placement. If I'm making more than one block, I reuse the same diamond shapes to do another mock-up.

TREE OF LIFE LAP QUILT

Size: 66″ × 66″

Total Big Blocks Needed: 4

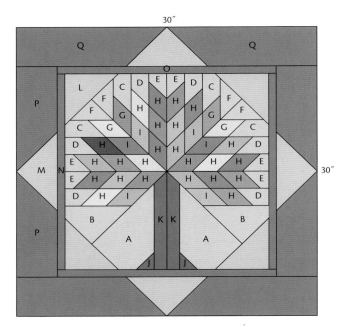

Big Block

Quilt Map

Complete Diagram

YARDAGE

ITEM	COLOR	QUANTITY NEEDED
Background (A,B,C,D,E,F)		3⅛ yards
Leaves (G, H, I)		¼ yard each of 12–14 different fabrics
Trunk (J, *K)		¼ yard
Triangles (L, M)		2⅛ yards
Lattice Strips (S),		
*Outer Border		
Inner Borders (N, O, P, Q, R)		2⅝ yards
Binding		¾ yard
Backing		72″ × 72″

*Based on cutting crosswise grain of the fabric. You will need to piece the borders to get the length required.

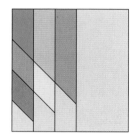

Unit 1; Make 8.

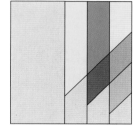

Unit 2; Make 8.

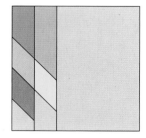

Unit 3A; Make 4.

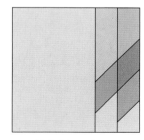

Unit 3B; Make 4.

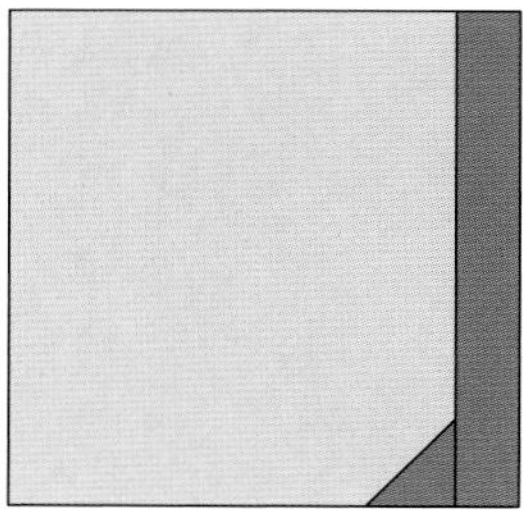

Unit 4A; Make 4.

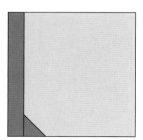

Unit 4B; Make 4.

CUTTING

ITEM	COLOR	# TO CUT	SIZE
A		8	9¼″ × 10½″
B		8	7″ × 10½″
C		16	2¼″ × 4½″
D		24	2¼″ × 3¾″
E		24	2¼″ × 3″
F		16	5¼″ × 10½″
G		16	2¼″ × 8¼″
H		96	2¼″ × 4¾″
I		24	2¼″ × 6½″
J		8	2¼″ × 2¼″
K		8	1¾″ × 10½″
L		16	5¾″ × 5¾″
M		16	4½″ × 8½″
N		8	1¼″ × 20½″
O		8	1¼″ × 22″
P		16	4½″ × 11¼″
Q		16	4½″ × 15¼″
R		1	2½″ × 2½″
S		4	2½″ × 30″
Borders		8	2¾″ × 40″

NOTE: For sewing instructions, see pages 76–79. Refer to the diagrams at left and below for the number of units and blocks needed.

Side Units; Make 8.

Top and Bottom Units; Make 8.

Big Block; Make 4.

TREE OF LIFE QUEEN/KING QUILT

(See photo on page 94.)

Queen: 97″ × 97″

King: 108″ × 108″

Big Blocks Needed: 9

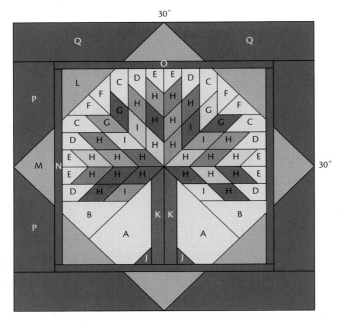

Big Block

Quilt Map

Complete Diagram

YARDAGE

ITEM	COLOR	Quantity Needed QUEEN	KING
Background (A, B, C, D, E, F)		6 yards	6 yards
Leaves (G, *H, I)		³⁄₈ yard of 12–14 different fabrics	³⁄₈ yard of 12–14 different fabrics
Trunk (J, *K)		½ yard	½ yard
Triangles (L, M)		4⅛ yards	6⅛ yards
Lattice Strips (S)			
*Outer Border			
Inner Borders (N, O, P, Q, R)		5½ yards	5½ yards
Binding		1 yard	1⅛ yards
Backing		103″ × 103″	114″ × 114″

*Based on cutting crosswise grain of the fabric. You will need to piece the borders to get the length required.

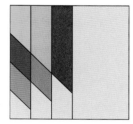

Unit 1; Make 18.

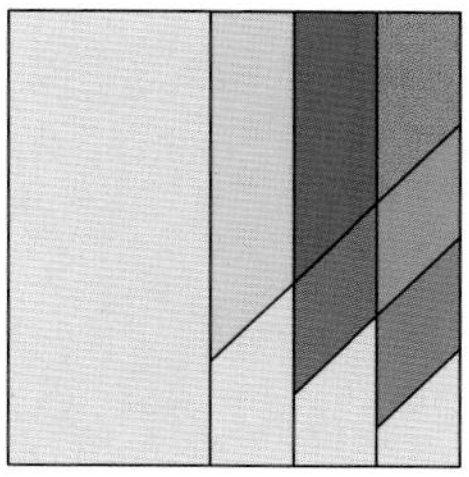

Unit 2; Make 18.

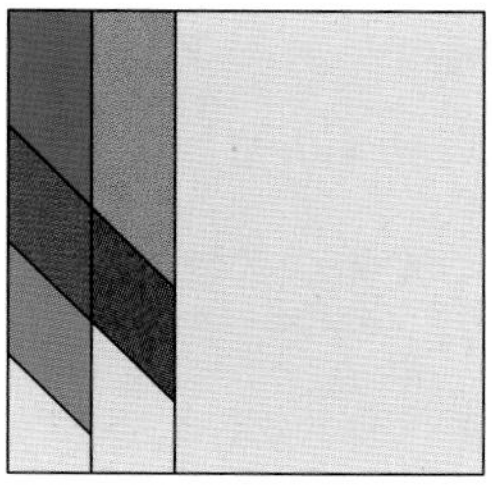

Unit 3A; Make 9.

Unit 3B; Make 9.

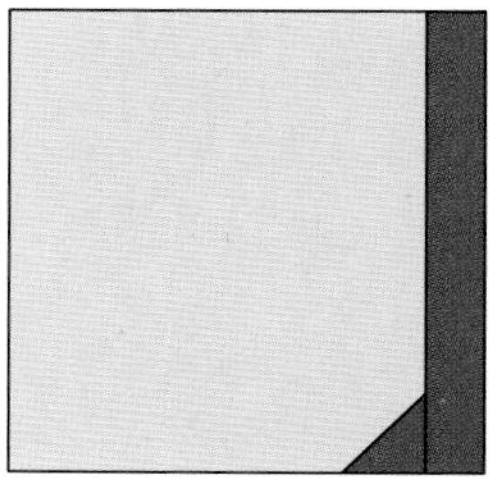

Unit 4A; Make 9.

Unit 4B; Make 9.

CUTTING for Queen and King

ITEM	COLOR	# TO CUT	SIZE
A		18	9¼″ × 10½″
B		18	7″ × 10½″
C		36	2¼″ × 4½″
D		54	2¼″ × 3¾″
E		54	2¼″ × 3″
F		36	5¼″ × 10½″
G		36	2¼″ × 8¼″
H		216	2¼″ × 4¾″
I		54	2¼″ × 6½″
J		18	2¼″ × 2¼″
K		18	1¾″ × 10½″
L		36	5¾″ × 5¾″
M		36	4½″ × 8½″
N		18	1¼″ × 20½″
O		18	1¼″ × 22″
P		36	4½″ × 11¼″
Q		36	4½″ × 15¼″
R		4	2½″ × 2½″
S		12	2½″ × 30″
Queen Borders		10	2½″ × 40″
King Borders		12	8″ × 40″

NOTE: For sewing instructions, see pages 76–79. Refer to the diagrams at left and below for the number of units and blocks needed.

Side Units; Make 18.

Top and Bottom Units; Make 18.

Big Block; Make 9.

PILLOWCASES

Pillowcases made by Nancy Johnson-Srebro.

Standard Size Pillowcase: $20^{3}/4'' \times 30''$

Queen Size Pillowcase: $20^{3}/4'' \times 34''$

King Size Pillowcase: $20^{3}/4'' \times 40''$

Each pillowcase takes only two rectangles of fabric to make! How easy is that? You can have fun embellishing them by adding lace, rickrack, buttons, or embroidery to the border (B).

These pillowcases are $3/4''$ wider and 4″ longer than purchased bed pillow forms. If you want to make them longer or shorter in length, just increase or decrease the length of the large rectangle (A).

 NO-FAIL TIPS

■ *You don't have to make matching pillowcases. The four pillowcases shown in the photo look wonderful together on a bed.*

■ *Use theme prints or holiday fabrics to make festive pillowcases that you can change with the seasons.*

YARDAGE for Two Pillowcases		Quantity Needed		
ITEM	COLOR	STANDARD	QUEEN	KING
Large Rectangle (A)		1⅝ yards	1⅞ yards	2¼ yards
*Border (B)		⅝ yard	⅝ yard	⅝ yard

*Based on cutting crosswise grain of the fabric.

STANDARD: $20^{3}/_{4}''$ × 30″

QUEEN: $20^{3}/_{4}''$ × 34″

KING: $20^{3}/_{4}''$ × 40″

NOTE: You must use fabric that is at least 42″ wide after selvages are removed.

CUTTING for Two Pillowcases			Standard	Queen	King
ITEM	COLOR	# TO CUT	SIZE	SIZE	SIZE
A		2	26½″ × 42″	30½″ × 42″	36½″ × 42″
B		2	8½″ × 42″	8½″ × 42″	8½″ × 42″

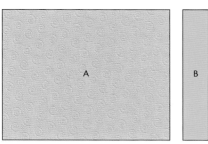

Assembly

Make 2.

Assembly

Step One

Fold B in half lengthwise with right sides together and press.

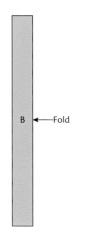

Make 2.

Step Two

Align the raw edges as shown and sew A to B using a ¼″ seam allowance. To reinforce this seam allowance, zig zag over it. Press the seam toward A.

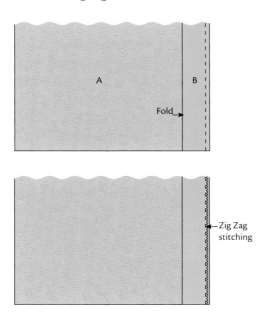

Make 2.

Step Three

Fold A/B in half lengthwise with right sides together and sew along the two sides using a ¼″ seam allowance. Zig zag the seam allowances. Make 2. Turn the pillowcases right side out.

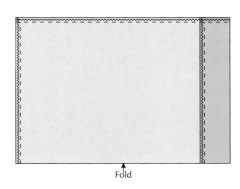

Fold

ACCENT PILLOWS

Pillows made by Nancy Johnson-Srebro.
Small Pillow: 24″ × 24″
Big Pillow: 30″ × 30″

These pillows are the ideal accent companions to the queen-and king-size quilts in this book. They're perfect for reading in bed, or toss a couple of them on the floor and you instantly have extra seating.

The crushed ruffle is fun to do and gives the pillows a very chic look. Make several to coordinate with each room in your house.

 NO-FAIL TIP

If you've been wanting to use your collection of large-print fabrics, now's your chance.
Warning: *Everyone who sees these pillows will want you to make one for them!*

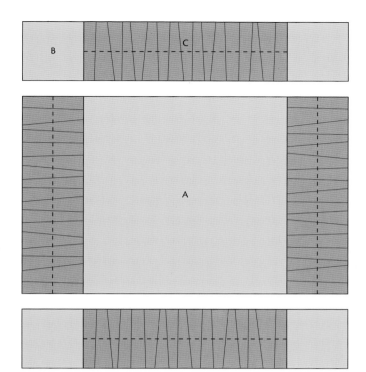

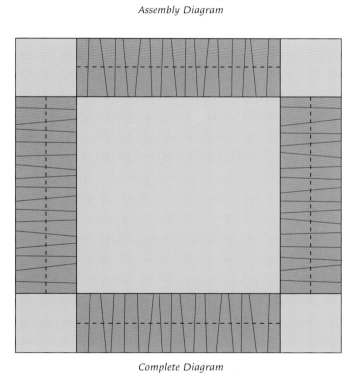

Assembly Diagram

Complete Diagram

YARDAGE AND MATERIAL   Quantity Needed

ITEM	COLOR	24″ PILLOW	30″ PILLOW
Center Square (A), Cornerstones (B), Backing		1¼ yards	1⅞ yards
*Crushed Ruffle (C)		⅞ yard	1⅛ yards
Pillow form		24″ × 24″	30″ × 30″

*Based on cutting crosswise grain of the fabric.

CUTTING

ITEM	COLOR	# TO CUT	24″ SIZE	30″ SIZE
A		1	16¼″ × 16¼″	19¼″ × 19¼″
B		4	5¾″ × 5¾″	7¼″ × 7¼″
C		4	5¾″ × 36″	7¼″ × 40″
Backing		2	17″ × 25¼″	21¼″ × 31¼″

NOTE: Use ⅝″ seam allowance throughout.

Make 2.

Make 2.

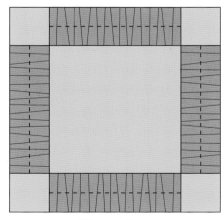

Pillow; Make 1.

Assembly

SEWING THE RUFFLE

Step One

Using a long basting stitch, sew ½" from the edge of the long side of C. Sew another row of basting stitches ⅝" from the same edge. Repeat on the opposite long side of C.

Step Two

To gather the strip, pull the bobbin threads until the length of the strip measures 16¼" for the 24" pillow or 19¼" for the 30" pillow.

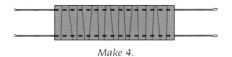

Make 4.

Step Three

After gathering the strips, set a hot iron on top of the first 6" of the strip to "crush" the gathers. Lift the iron and repeat for another 6". Keep doing this until you reach the other end. Do not move the iron back and forth on the strip.

To sew the crushed gathers in place, measure in 2⅞" from the long edge for the 24" pillow and sew over the crushed gathers using a standard stitch length. For the 30" pillow, measure in 3⅝". You can use a decorative stitch to sew the gathers in place if desired.

> **✳ *Easy Sewing Guide***
> *Place a piece of ¼" masking tape down the center of the strip and sew along that.*

SEWING THE PILLOW FRONT

Step One

Sew a crushed ruffle to opposite sides of the center square (A), using a ⅝" seam allowance.

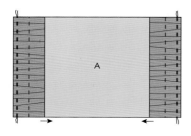

Step Two

Sew the remaining 2 crushed ruffle strips to the B corner squares.

Sew to the top and bottom of the unit from Step One.

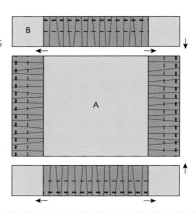

MAKING THE PILLOW BACK

Step One

Hem the inner edges (a longer side) of the 2 backing panels.

Step Two

Overlap the 2 backing pieces so they measure 25¼" × 25¼" for the 24" pillow or 31¼" × 31¼" for the 30" pillow. Pin and baste along the top and bottom edges.

Step Three

With right sides together, stitch the pillow front to the pillow back using a ⅝" seam allowance. Turn the pillow covering right side out. Insert the pillow form.

Indian Cartwheels

Lap Quilt Size: 52″ × 52″

Made by Nancy Johnson-Srebro.

Quilted by Veronica Nurmi.

Perennial spring colors make this an appealing quilt no matter what the season.

Summer in the Neighborhood

Lap Quilt Size: $63\frac{1}{2}'' \times 59''$

Made by Nancy Johnson-Srebro.

Quilted by Veronica Nurmi.

If you're fond of house blocks, this one is for you.
Two house blocks, four trees, and you're done!

Baskets on the Landing

Lap Quilt Size: 52″ × 52″

Made by Nancy Johnson-Srebro.

Quilted by Veronica Nurmi.

This simple and elegant quilt with baskets of a lovely floral print could take on just about any personality, depending on your fabric choices.

Market Square
Lap Quilt Size: 48″ × 48″
Made by Nancy Johnson-Srebro.
Quilted by Veronica Nurmi.

The bold, graphic lines and strong colors make this a rich and fascinating quilt, subject to interpretation in your own favorite colors.

Make Mine Rickrack
Queen Size: 96″ × 96″
Made by Nancy Johnson-Srebro.
Quilted by Cindy Needham.

Here's a fabulous traditional quilt with a fun twist that gives the look of old-fashioned rickrack. Rickrack and stars… what could be better?!

Carolina Lily All Grown Up

Queen Size: 94″ × 104″

Made by Nancy Johnson-Srebro.

Quilted by Veronica Nurmi.

Pinwheels dance around four lovely lily blocks in fresh, bright eye-catching colors.

Shade Trees of Life

Queen Size: 97″ × 97″

Made by Nancy Johnson-Srebro.

Quilted by Veronica Nurmi.

Using light and darker shades of the same colors around the trees adds depth and provides an intriguing illusion of transparency. The trees seem to be surrounded by light and shadow.

RESOURCES

American & Efird, Inc.
Consumer Division
P.O. Box 507
Mt. Holly, NC 28120
www.amefird.com

Bernina of America
3702 Prairie Lake Drive
Aurora, IL 60504
www.berninausa.com

Fairfield Processing Corp.
www.poly-fil.com

FreeSpirit
1350 Broadway
21st Floor
New York, NY 10018
www.freespiritfabric.com

Hobbs Bonded Fibers
P.O. Box 2521
Waco, TX 76702
www.hobbsbondedfibers.com

Mountain Mist
2551 Crescentville Road
Cincinnati, OH 45241
www.mountainmist@leggett.com

P&B Textiles
1580 Gilbreth Road
Burlingame, CA 94010
www.pbtex.com

Prym Consumer USA Inc.
Spartanburg, SC 29304
www.dritz.com
www.omnigrid.com

RJR Fashion Fabrics
2203 Dominguez Street
Torrance, CA 90501
www.rjrfabrics.com

Robert Kaufman Co, Inc.
129 W. 132nd Street
Los Angeles, CA 90061
www.robertkaufman.com

Superior Threads
P.O. Box 1672
St. George, UT 84771
www.superiorthreads.com

Timeless Treasures
483 Broadway
New York, NY 10013
www.ttfabrics.com

The Warm Company
954 E. Union Street
Seattle, WA 98122
www.warmcompany.com

QUILTING STENCILS

All stencils used in the quilts are available from:

Quilting Creations International
P.O. Box 512
Zoar, OH 44697
www.quiltingcreations.com

Indian Puzzle, Option A (page 13): Stencil #592 was used in the border.

Indian Puzzle, Option B (page 13): Stencil #VN67 was enlarged to 15" and used in the center of the quilt.

Rick Rack and Roll, Option B (page 23): Stencils #NH116 and #287 were used to create the center wreath design.

Baskets, Option A (page 31): Stencil #VN56 was used in the center of the basket bottom and #VN60 was used in the borders.

Home Sweet Home, Option A (page 32): Stencil #VN63, free-motion stars and swirls, was used in the background.

Carolina Lily, Option A (page 61): Stencil #160 was used for the border design.

Carolina Lily, Option B (page 61): Stencil #NH15 was used as the basis for the quilting design shown in the corners of the lily block and #NH3000-B1 was used for the border.

Tree of Life, Option A (page 73): Stencil #VN18 was used in the border area around the tree.

Tree of Life, Option B (page 73): Stencil #VN17 was used in the center of the tree. The stencil for the cable shown is #65, and #VN138 was used in the outer border.

ABOUT THE AUTHOR

Grandma Garrison was Nancy's mentor while she made her first quilt in 1972. She asked her to cut a 6" square template from paper and pin it on some fabric. Using regular scissors, quite dull, Nancy cut around the paper template. After cutting about two dozen squares, she noticed some of the squares were not the same size. Nancy called Gram and said, "My blocks don't seem to be the same size." Gram replied, "Are you cutting any of the paper template off when you cut around it?" Nancy replied, "No, only once in a while!" That was Nancy's first lesson in accuracy and it has stuck with her all these years. Today her hallmark is accuracy and she stresses it with students and attributes the wide recognition of her work to its continued emphasis.

She has written several best-selling books including *Featherweight 221: The Perfect Portable®*, and *Rotary Magic*. Nancy also refined how to work with squares and rectangles in her other best selling books *Block Magic*, *Block Magic, Too!*, and *Stars by Magic*.

Nancy has been a spokesperson for Omnigrid, a division of Prym Consumer USA, Inc., for over 16 years.

Nancy lives in Pennsylvania with her husband, Frank. They have three grown children and one granddaughter. She travels extensively to teach and lecture on the wonderful art of quiltmaking. You can learn more about Nancy at www.nancyjohnsonsrebro.com.

Other titles by Nancy:

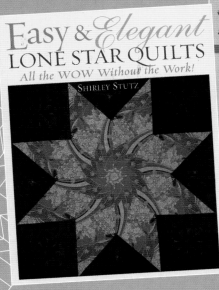

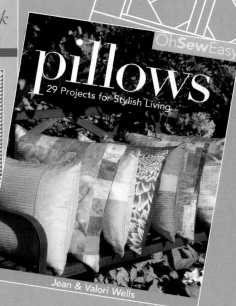